HARDPRESS.NET
HOME OF HARD-TO-FIND BOOKS

The Ellis Correspondence
by John Ellis

Address:
HardPress
8345 NW 66TH ST #2561
MIAMI FL 33166-2626
USA
Email: info@hardpress.net

THE

ELLIS CORRESPONDENCE.

VOL. II.

LONDON:
PRINTED BY S. AND R. BENTLEY,
Dorset Street, Fleet Street.

THE

ELLIS CORRESPONDENCE.

LETTERS

WRITTEN DURING THE YEARS 1686, 1687, 1688,

AND ADDRESSED TO JOHN ELLIS, ESQ.

SECRETARY TO THE COMMISSIONERS OF HIS MAJESTY'S REVENUE IN IRELAND:

COMPRISING MANY PARTICULARS OF

THE REVOLUTION,

AND ANECDOTES ILLUSTRATIVE OF THE HISTORY AND
MANNERS OF THOSE TIMES.

EDITED, FROM THE ORIGINALS, WITH NOTES AND A PREFACE,

BY THE HON. GEORGE AGAR ELLIS.

IN TWO VOLUMES.

VOL. II.

LONDON:
HENRY COLBURN, NEW BURLINGTON STREET.
1829.

CONTENTS

OF THE SECOND VOLUME.

LETTERS,

&c.

CXXXVIII.

The King at Hounslow.—The Jury to try the Bishops.—
Other news.

London, June 28th, 1688.

SIR,

HIS Majesty was pleased yesterday to go to Hounslow Heath, where the camp opened, and a battalion of the guards marched. His Majesty did the Lord Churchill * the honour to dine in his tent. In his return, he called at Richmond, and viewed the Palace, where the Prince of Wales is to be lodged, as the Prince

* John Lord Churchill, afterwards the great Duke of Marlborough.

VOL. II.   B

and Princess of Denmark are to be at Hampton Court.

To-morrow (though St. Peter's day) being the day for the trial of the seven Bishops, preparations are making for it accordingly : it is a bad wind that blows nobody good. The officers of the Court will get well by the trial for places and conveniences to hear the same, which are sold excessively dear. Most of the nobility are also come up, and will be present. The panel of the jury, as it was agreed on, is as followeth :—

Sir Roger Langley.   Rich. Shoreditch.
Sir John Berry.   Wm. Hewer.
Sir William Hill.   Nich. Baxter.
Roger Jennings.   Nehemiah Arnold.
Tho. Harriott.   John Greene.
Geoffry Nightingale.   Rob. Burre.
Wm. Wither.   Geo. Ford.
Wm. Avery.   Char. Prior.
Tho. Austine.   Ed. Harris.
Nich. Griev.   John Walton.
ʃ Mich. Arnold.   James Supple.
Tho. Donne.   Rich. Cooper.

Of which the twelve first will likely stand for a jury, in case they do appear, unless some very legal objection be made against them. Most of them are known to be Church-of-England-men : several are employed by the King in his navy and revenue ; and some are, or once were, of the Dissenters' party.

On the 26th, Mr. Attorney General * prayed judgment against several Charters and Corporations in England and Wales, that are forfeited, for not pleading to the *Quo Warranto* brought against them.

Mr. Boyle, the dancing-master, who was lately convicted at the Old Bailey of having seditious views, moved for a writ of error ; but it being debated whether such a writ lay or no, the Court was of the negative opinion ; and the matter is referred to the Attorney General.

One La Mar, a Frenchman, and one Blamer, were brought up to the Court of King's Bench,

---

* Sir Thomas Powis. Burnet calls him " a compliant, young, aspiring lawyer." He had lately succeeded Sir Robert Sawyer, who was turned out for refusing to support the King's dispensing power.

to plead to an information of breaking open the Royal Oak Lottery-box, but were remanded again to Newgate.

We expect verses gratulatory upon the birth of the Prince from both the Universities, and also from the society of Magdalen College, in Oxford, in a particular book by themselves.

We are told from Oxford, that the Convocation voted against an Act; only Obadiah Walker* and some of his friends were for it. Cambridge seems also inclined to have no Commencement, but it is not yet determined.

Our French letters tell us of the arrival of the French fleet before Algiers, so that an account of their performances is impatiently expected.

The Count de Grammont† is dispatched by

---

* Obadiah Walker, head of University College, Oxford. He had become a Roman Catholic in the year 1686. The Universities were anxious to have no public ceremonies, as a mark of their sorrow at the state of the times.

† Philibert Count de Grammont, brother of the Marshal of that name, but best known as the hero of the Memoires de Grammont, written by Count Anthony Hamilton. He lived

the most Christian King to compliment the Court of England upon the birth of the Prince.

For John Ellis, Esq. Secretary to the
   Commissioners for the Revenue of
   Ireland,
                     At Dublin.

CXXXIX.

The Bishops acquitted.

30th June, 1688.

THE inclosed gives a pretty true, though but a general account of ten hours labour; Spence may add somewhat more. It was five this morning before the Jury agreed their verdict; Arnold, the brewer, is said to have held out so long. About thirty temporal Lords attended; but the crowd and the rabble, the shouts and huzzas yesterday, and the *Io triumphe's* to-day were incredible.* The Solicitor-

to repent of the errors and vices of his youth, and died at the age of eighty-six, January 10th, 1707.

* " The news of the Bishops being acquitted was received

general* kept his ground against Finch, Sawyer, Pemberton, Pollexfen, Levinz, Treby,† and Somers,‡ with great assurance, and spared none when they came within his circle and reach.

Mr. Ellis.

with the highest expressions of joy throughout the whole kingdom ; nor could the King's own presence prevent his army, that was then encamped at Hounslow Heath, from mixing their loud acclamations with the rest. This last mortification might have prevented his fate, if his ears had been open to any but a hot party, that were positively resolved to push for all, cost what it would."—Welwood's Memoirs.

* Sir William Williams. Burnet says the cause against the Bishops was principally managed by him. He calls him " a corrupt and vicious man, who had no principles, but followed his own interests." And adds, " Powis (Attorney-General) acted his part in this trial as fairly as his post could admit of. But Williams took very indecent liberties."

† Sir George Treby. Evelyn calls him " a learned man in his profession." He was made Attorney-General in 1689, and Chief Justice of the Common Pleas in 1692. He died in 1701.

‡ Afterwards the great Lord Somers. " One of those divine men," to use the expressions of Horace Walpole, " who, like a chapel in a palace, remain unprofaned, while all the rest is tyranny, corruption, and folly."

CXL.

Details respecting the Trial of the Bishops.

London, June 30th, 1688.

SIR,

YESTERDAY the seven Bishops came to their trial, which held from morning till seven at night. We gave you an account of the jury in our last. The first twelve stood, only Sir John Berry was not there : they did not bring in their verdict last night, and it is said they had not agreed upon it this day at four in the morning.

The Counsel, in handling the matter for the Bishops, divided the substance of the information into two parts, whereof the same consisted ; the first was, that they had maliciously, seditiously, and slanderously made, contrived, and published, a false and seditious libel against the King, which tended to diminish his regal authority and prerogative : the second part of the plea for the Bishops was as to the special matter of their petition, which showed there was no malice or sedition in it.

As to the first point, much time was spent in proving the hands of the Bishops: that of the Archbishop was proved and well known by several; but that of the other Bishops was not otherwise made out than by the belief and supposition of the witnesses, though their own servants were subpœnaed against their masters, so that the Court was of opinion there was not sufficient proof of their hand-writing.

As to the Archbishop, it was objected, that he could not be within the indictment, for that it was laid in Middlesex, and his Grace had not been out of Surrey in seven or eight months. To this it was answered, that his signing and writing of the petition, and sending of it over to be delivered in Middlesex, was a sufficient publishing of it there. But the Court was divided in this point.

Then the King's Counsel alledged, that the Bishops had owned their hand-writing in the Council, and had also confessed the delivery of the petition. It was replied, on the Bishops' side, that they had owned their hands, but after that the Lord Chancellor had required them to do it; and that they had done it, trusting to his Majesty's goodness that no advantage would be made of their confession against themselves. But they denied they had owned the delivery of the petition, much less that they had published it; and there being no other evidence of it than that they had been with the Lord Sunderland, and had offered his Lordship a sight of a petition, which he had refused, nor did he see them deliver it to the King, the Court said it was only a presumption, and no proof.

As to the matter of the petition, whether a libel upon the Government or no, the Attorney and Solicitor-general maintained it was; for that it boldly meddled with the acts of the Government, declaring his Majesty's toleration to be illegal, and thereby tending to diminish the King's authority and prerogative royal.

To this the Bishops' Counsel replied, that they

had done but what was the right of every subject, to petition the King, and that in matter of conscience, and upon the account of religion, which they were by their oaths and by the laws of the land to take care of; and quoted several laws and statutes to that purpose. They urged also, that they did not declare the King's Declaration of indulgence to be illegal, but said only that the Parliaments of 62, 72, and 89, had declared so; whereupon the Journals of Lords and Commons were read.

The Court was also divided in this point. The Chief Justice and Judge Allibone said that it was a libel, but Judges Powell and Holloway were of a contrary opinion.*

The Attorney and Solicitor were only for the King, and kept their ground against Pem-

* " The Counsel for the Bishops, the ablest of their profession in all England, produced such arguments in their behalf, that the judges were divided, two of them declaring that the proofs did not extend to the making their petition or address a libel, and two of them that they did, which cost Sir Richard Holloway and Sir John Powell their seats on the bench as soon as the term was over."—Reresby's Memoirs.

berton, Sawyer, Finch, Pollexfen, Treby, and Sommers, who were for the Bishops.

This morning, between ten and eleven, the Jury brought in their verdict, the Bishops attending in Court, Not Guilty in part or whole: which causes great joy.

For John Ellis, Esq. Secretary to the
   Commissioners for the Revenue of
   Ireland,   At Dublin.

CXLI.

Farther details respecting the Trial.—Other news.

London, July 3d, 1688.

SIR,

THE Jury having brought in their verdict of Not Guilty upon the Bishops on Saturday morning, the unruly *mobile* broke out into wild huzzas and acclamations: some of the gown were also observed to be as loud as any, for which the Attorney-general caused one of Gray's Inn to be seized, and bound him to answer to an information.   The Solicitor-general was like to catch another, but that he narrowly escaped in the crowd.

The giddy rabble continued their disorderly joys till Sunday morning, making bonfires all Saturday night, and committing some insolencies where they found no contributions; several were wounded, others were robbed, and many will be called to an account this week that the Quarter Sessions do begin.

Yesterday the Lord Mayor appeared before the King and his Council, to give account of those few bonfires which were made in the City by some of too fiery and indiscreet zeal.*

* " Westminster Hall, the Palace Yards, and all the streets about, were thronged with an infinite people, whose loud shouts and joyful acclamations upon hearing the Bishops were acquitted, were a very rebellion in noise, though very far from so either in fact or intention.   Bonfires were made, not only in the City of London, but in most towns in England, as soon as the news reached them; though there were strict and general orders given out to prevent all such doings; and the clergy preached more loudly and more freely than ever against the errors of the Latin church.   The

His Majesty hath granted out a commission to the Earl of Rochester, Governor of the Merchant Adventurers of England, and to several others, to inspect and regulate the woollen trade, and to give orders to prevent the exportation of wool.

Mr. Tipping, of Oxfordshire, was fined 5000*l.* for having contrived the marriage of one Silverlock, a young gentleman of 1500*l.* a year, (to whom the said Tipping was guardian,) with a punk of his own, promising the relations of the young Esquire she was a fortune, and should be with him 7 or 8000*l.* Tipping hath been fled into Holland these two years, for this piece of ingenuity.

One Upmar, a famous kidnapper, was convicted and fined but 20*s.*, for that he gives evidence, and makes discovery against others, so

next day I waited on the King to the camp on Hounslow Heath, where every body observed him to labour under a very great disturbance of mind ; but he spoke very kindly to me, as I rode by him upon several occasions."—Reresby's Memoirs.

that sometimes the greatest offender hath the greatest merit, if he be but ingenious.

We are very suddenly to expect out a proclamation against debaucheries and sabbath-breakers: it comes out so slowly, for that it is to pass through many hands that are concerned in it. It curbs even our loose houses, and regulates our very sleeping ; and the good wives are well-wishers to it, for that it obliges men and masters to keep good hours, and go to bed betimes.

We hear that Esquire Sheridan doth appear (though not very publicly) at Court ; and that he is to be remanded back again into Ireland ; the farther prosecution of his affairs being left to the law of that kingdom.

Lady Ivy and Mr. Neale had another trial yesterday at the Bench of Common Pleas, where several things were given in evidence, on both sides, of a very odd nature, touching forging of deeds and conveyances. The jury are to give in their verdict this day.

The same Mr. Neale has lately received a

considerable loss by a fire that happened a day or two ago at Tunbridge.

Lord Chancellor and William Penn were plaintiffs in a cause, about a lease, against the Lady Herbert, defendant; the Court of King's Bench have remitted the said cause to be determined by my Lord Chancellor himself, who offered the lady a considerable sum of money.

An appeal is brought against one Walter Vincent, for killing the husband of one Mrs. Killegrew; and the Earl of Radnor * and the Lord Chandois † were his bail.

The business of the King's Bench Prison, between the Lord Hunsdon,‡ on behalf of the King, and Mr. Louthall, is put off till the

* Charles Bodville (Robartes) second Earl of Radnor. He married the daughter of Sir John Cutler, the celebrated miser, and died s. p. in 1723.

† James (Bridges) eighth Lord Chandos; sometime Ambassador at Constantinople. He married Elizabeth, daughter of Sir Henry Bernard, Knight, by whom he became the father of twenty-two children.

‡ Robert (Carey) sixth Lord Hunsdon: succeeded to that title on the death of John fifth Lord Hunsdon and second Earl of Dover, in 1677. He died in France, in 1692.

next term: and Mr. Ellis, the new Marshal, put in by Mr. Louthall, is to give security to answer the profits of the place in the mean time.

Some of our last German letters seem to threaten us with the loss of the Duke of Lorrain, giving suspicions of poison, and despairing of his recovery; others again enliven us with hopes that the danger is over, and that he may yet take the field this campaign.

For John Ellis, Esq. Secretary to the
   Commissioners for the Revenue
   of Ireland,
                    At Dublin.

CXLII.

The King desires persons holding office to come into Parliament, &c.

July 5th, 1688.

DEAR MR. ELLIS,

Though I have given you no trouble by way of letter since my arrival at London, yet I will assure you no day has passed without some thoughts concerning you, and my perpetual wishes of seeing you here, has been the true reason why I have not writ to you sooner. The truth is, I had writ to you long time since about a little affair of my own, that is, to have got my licence enlarged : but Mr. Cullyford undertook that affair, and through multitude of business slipt it. He has promised me this post to make amends, and write to you effectually about it ; and if he fails, I shall call him to an account for it anon over a bottle, when we give your health. Mr. Dickinson arrived here last week : he looks extremely well as ever I saw him. Mr. C. and he, and I, Mr. Kitely, Mr. Sangrove, dined together on Saturday, where you were not forgot. Honest Mr. Sangrove dropped a word that your ink was made of very sharp vinegar, but nothing could oblige him to interpret it ; so the jest was lost, and so perhaps it may be to you.

He was yesterday with the Lords of the Treasury, the King present, who immediately called for him up, received him with all ima-

ginable kindness, thanked him publicly for his
good service in Ireland, told him my Lord
Deputy·had writ so very kindly that he knew
how to believe enough of him, but withal added, that though he gave him very willingly
leave to stay his own time to attend his own
affairs, yet he both designed and commanded
him to return as soon as possible to his post
in Ireland : but things of this nature I know
you have from better hands.   I think fit, by
the way, to let you know that when I applied
to Mr. Dickinson about this matter, he assured
me, upon his word, he had the Commissioners'
consent for my stay here till his return, and
that I should wait on him back ; and you know
what an impudent thing it would be in me to
take his word for a compliment.   I will now
give you the true reason why I am so zealous
in this matter, and leave it to you to be my
judge as well as my advocate.   My cousin
Cooke is a man very subject to melancholy fits ;
he has had some formerly upon less occasions,
but is now teazed with me upon the loss of his

former trade, and the little prospect there is that it shall ever return; and it is a necessity for him to retire somewhere till time, which is the only cure, has mended him, and which he will not do without me, and the truth of this Mr. C. knows very well. After this story, I am sure I need not desire you to present my duty to the Commissioners, and to procure a formal enlargement of my licence, if it be necessary, and to sweeten Mr. Strong apart, from whom I only apprehend, and yet I hope it is without reason. Dear Sir, excuse this trouble, and draw a bill of ten times as much upon me here, and I will pay it at sight; and if you please to send me word how it is reported, you will oblige me extraordinarily.

I have told you of Mr. Dickinson already. There was at the same time my Lord Ranelagh,* Mr. Cullyford, Mr. Kent, to whom my

* Richard (Jones) Viscount Ranelagh in Ireland, created Earl of Ranelagh in 1677. He sat long in the English Parliament. He was at this time Paymaster to the Army. He died January 5th, 1711.

Lord Godolphine addressed in this manner;—
" My Lord, the King commands you to stand
for Parliament-man at Plymouth : you, Mr. C.
at Cork ; and you, Mr. Kent, at your own town."
My Lord said he was made by my Lord of
Bathe,* and did not know one person in that
town : it was answered, the King's interest
shall supply that.   Mr. C. answered, that it was
true he had once an interest, but that there had
been two Parliaments since his being upon the
place, and that he was well informed the country gentry would approve at every election,
which would make the charge extravagant : it
was answered the King would take care of
that.   Mr. Kent made the same excuse, and
had the same return.   I tell you this long
story (which pray keep to yourself,) that you
may see there will certainly be a Parliament in
November.   Mr. Kitely's business hangs still ;
the King unwilling to break his word.   E.
Peters will not admit an apostate to prefer-

---

* Lord Ranelagh had been returned for Plymouth, upon
the interest of Granville Earl of Bath.

ment. Mr. T., the person designed, is very well here, and cannot be prevailed upon to accept it. Mr. K. has had a very kind message from the King by my Lord of Dover, that he should not be impatient, nor give over his pretensions to what he was about, for if he were not pre-ferred this bout, he should be sooner than he expected ; and this is all I know of your Eng-lish-Irish affairs. I have nothing left but to renew my request to you to transact my little affair with your own prudence, and then I am sure it will succeed, and rather than not hear from you, let me have a taste of your vinegar, raillery apart. I can be no more yours

Than I am,

Sir, your most

Obliged and faithful

Humble servant,

FRA. CAVE.

My Governor and I and Mr. C. are going to dine and drink your health.

(No address on this Letter.)

CXLIII.

7th July, 1688.

SIR,

WE have three new Judges made, or to be made.   Serjeant Ingoldsby, to be Baron of the Exchequer, instead of Powell, who, with Serjeant Baldock, are to supply the cushions in the King's Bench of the other Powell and Holloway, who are *quietus'd.*   Serjeant Rotheram comes to the Common Pleas in the seat of either Street or Milton, who is very old.*   Great expectations there are of other changes in the Long Robe, but no manner of certainty.

(No address on this Letter.)

-----

* The law changes at this time were as follows.   Sir Robert Baldock, who was one of the King's Counsel on the trial, succeeded Sir John Powell; and Sir Thomas Powell succeeded Sir Richard Holloway.   Sir Christopher Milton, one of the Judges of the Common Pleas, was succeeded by Sir Thomas Jenner, and Serjeant Ingleby and Serjeant Rotherham were made Barons of the Exchequer.

CXLIV.

New Privy Councillors made.—Prince of Wales ordered to be prayed for.—Various rumours.—Foreign news.

London, July 7th, 1688.

SIR,

LAST night his Majesty was pleased to admit of his Most Honourable Privy Council these persons following, viz. Sir John Trevor, Knight, Master of the Rolls, Mr. Sylas Titus,* (commonly called Colonel Titus,) and Christo-

---

* Silas Titus was the author of the celebrated pamphlet of " Killing no Murder," of which the object was to incite persons to the assassination of Cromwell. He was also himself one of those who were employed by Clarendon, (see Clarendon State Papers,) to effect the murder of the Protector : a scheme which was only given up in consequence of the death of that eminent man by natural means. He was a mere adventurer, and served, at different times of his life, all sides and all parties. Swift calls him " the greatest rogue in England." He was born about 1622, and died during the reign of King William. He was first a captain in the Parliament army, and afterwards Groom of the Bedchamber to Charles the Second. He was a great supporter of Titus Oates, and the Popish Plot : in spite of which, as we see by the text, James made him a Privy Councillor. He was long a member of the House of Commons.

pher Vane,* Esquire, son of the late Sir Henry Vane, a person of good estate in the county of Durham.†

His Majesty is so much pleased with the care and ability of Sir Wm. Williams, his Solicitor-general, particularly in his late behaviour about the trial of the Bishops, that he has been pleased to confer the honour of a Baronet upon him.

His Majesty dines at the camp most commonly twice a week, as he did last Wednesday with Major-general Worden, where there were eight regiments of horse, besides six or seven thousand foot drawn up.

* Christopher Vane, eldest son of " young Sir Harry Vane," who was beheaded for High Treason, June 11th, 1662.   This Christopher was created Lord Barnard in 1699. He married Elizabeth Holles, one of the sisters and coheiresses of John (Holles) Duke of Newcastle, and died October 28th, 1723.

† The entry in the Diary of Henry Lord Clarendon, with regard to these admissions to the Privy Council, is as follows :

" July 6th, Sir John Trevor, Master of the Rolls, Colonel Tytus, and Mr. Vane, Sir Henry Vane's son, were sworn of the Privy Council.   Good God bless us ! what will the world come to !"

Their Majesties and the Prince continue in very good health. The King hath declared the Prince, Prince of Wales, though he is not yet created, and hath ordered him to be prayed for in all churches under that title. About fifteen days hence the Court will be removing to Windsor, and the Prince to Richmond.

About the 10th of this month, the Queen's Majesty intends to come abroad, her month being then out; and to welcome her Majesty there are eight or nine vast engines made upon the Thames, of different forms and figures, which are to play several sorts of fireworks within a few nights after.

His Majesty's squadron of ships, being about twenty-six strong with the fireships, are, all but two, said to be sailed from the Downs towards Sole Bay; and some think his Majesty may speedily go down the river to take a view of them. We hear no more of the French squadron, nor the Dutch fleet, besides what their prints tell us, that they are to be speedily forty sail in number.

Since the trial of the Bishops, Sir Richard Holloway and Sir John Powell, two of the Judges of the King's Bench Court, have had their *Quietus* sent them ; and it is credibly reported that Serjeant Boldock and Serjeant Trinder (one of those newly made), both which were of counsel for the King at the trial of the Bishops, will be made Judges in the others' stead.

It is commonly discoursed that there are some other changes to be in Westminster Hall ; and if so, it is generally believed that his Majesty will have a gracious regard to the merits and great capacities of Sir Wm. Williams, his Solicitor-general.

What is surmised of a farther trial intended against the Bishops before the Lords Ecclesiastical, is yet uncertain, there being no citations yet gone out against them.

A great many other surmises and uncertainties are invented, and industriously spread about the coffee-houses of our town, touching his Majesty's ministers and his affairs, but very often what is most generally reported proves most false.

The Duke of Lorrain's indisposition has not only kept back the operations of the German campaign, but in great measure made others less inquisitive after the success of it. That Duke's illness and relapse, the refusal of the Elector of Bavaria to command this campaign, and the late vast overflowing of the Drave and Save, seem to be so contrived as if it were an intimation given the Emperor from above, that it is high time to set boundaries to his conquest, and to keep what he has already got; and to that end, Fortune seems to have designed a very easy conquest of those few places still remaining to the Turks in Hungary; for Count Caraffa no sooner appeared before Lippa, a strong garrison upon Marosh, but the town yielded at discretion, though there were five thousand men in garrison.

The Queen Duchess of Lorrain* was sent for post to Vienna upon the relapse of the

* Eleanor, sister of the Emperor Leopold, and widow of

Duke.   The little hopes the physicians gave her of his life made her disconsolate ;. and what more distracted the Emperor's Council was, factions and divisions that were like to grow in the army, by the absence of the two Dukes.*

The boors and countrymen about Canissa have desired the Emperor to employ his troops elsewhere, and to give them leave to reap the honour of taking that place, which they may the easier do, it being already half starved, and there being but one causeway to lead provisions into it.

There is the old struggling at Cologn for the Electorship ; and the Cardinal of Furstembergh's pretensions are the more perplexed, since that the Pope has granted two briefs in favour of his competitors.

For John Ellis, Esq. Secretary to the
  Commissioners for the Revenue of
  Ireland.   at Dublin.

Michael Wiecnowiecki, King of Poland ; re-married to Charles the Fifth, Duke of Lorraine.
  * Of Bavaria and Lorraine.

CXLV.

Various trials.—Sir John Narborough and the Duke of Albemarle.—Magdalen College.—Prince of Wales gives au-
diences, &c.

London, July 8th, 1688.

SIR,

THE term is now ended, but by the
shortness of it, several businesses were put off
till the next term ; as, the dispute between the
Lord Hunsdon and Mr. Louthall, about the
Mastership of the King's Bench Office ; nor
did the Court pronounce judgment in the case
of the *Quo Warranto's*, but hath put it off till
it be argued again.

Mr. Neal hath gained a verdict against the
Lady Ivy at last, as she did against him once
or twice before ; and some think the question
about the forged writings may again be stirred.

The twelve Judges have considered the plea
of Charles Deering, Esq. upon the appeal of
Mrs. Goring ; and all were of opinion that the
plea was nought, except Judge Street.

The fine of 5000*l.* imposed upon Mr. Tipping, mentioned in my last, was argued again, and the question seemed to be, whether he, being outlawed, and so having forfeited all he hath to the King, ought to be fined besides: it is put off to a farther day.

Since the trial of the Bishops, it has been commonly discoursed as if the Judges Holloway and Powell were to have their *Quietus,* and that Serjeant Boldock and Trinder are to succeed them: a few days may clear the point.

Sir John Narborough is still a-fishing upon the Spanish wreck, and is said not to have recovered above 20 or 30,000*l.* by reason that there lies a prodigious quantity of indigo and coral, which covers the silver, and it being in deep water, cannot be so easily cleaned by the divers.

The Duke of Albemarle is said to have discovered a mine of silver in Jamaica, and most of his Grace's family have had the good luck to win at play very large sums from several in the island, that had been a-fishing upon the wreck, so that they parted with it freely as they found it.

The new society of Magdalen College in Oxford, having examined the treasury of the College, found among other things, 300 pieces of old gold, but with this injunction of the founder, that that money is not to be employed any way but in repairing of the College, in case of fire.

The talk of the coffee-houses will have it, that the Lords Commissioners Ecclesiastical are to take some of the clergy to task for not reading the Declaration ; others will have it, that a new proclamation will issue out to order the reading of it again : but all this is uncertain.

The Prince is in very good health, and hath given audience to several foreign ministers ; the Lord Mayor of York is come to town to kiss the Prince's hand, and to present him a purse of gold, as the Lord Mayor of London did.

The Queen is in public again, and is to name a day for the fire-works on the River.

For John Ellis, Esq. Secretary to the
 Commissioners for the Revenue of
 Ireland,
　　　　　　　　At Dublin.

CXLVI.

London, July 10th, 1688.

DEAR SIR,

I AM just returned from a Western expedition of five weeks, where my time was
somewhat better spent than last year. I found
yours at my return, of the 5th of last month,
and my Prior alive now, learning to crawl;
your Bishop* with him taking Kensington air.
*Many alterations talked on in our Court. Two
new Privy Councillors on Friday next : Caryll,
the Queen's Secretary, and Major Bremer.
The young Prince† is ill, but it is a secret. I
think he will not hold, and that must be the less
so for being a general opinion.*

Yours,

J. F.

Mr. Ellis.

The Foreign Ministers Zulestein and Count

---

* Philip Ellis.
† The Prince of Wales.

Grammont stay to see the issue, and there is more than one in being.

Let yours hereafter be left for me with Mr. James Dalton at the General Post Office.

For John Ellis, Esq. Secretary of His
  Majesty's Revenue in Ireland.
Ireland.   Dublin.

CXLVII.

Reported changes in the Law.—Their Majesties going to Windsor.—Foreign news.

London, July 10th, 1688
SIR,

THE many reports which were lately spread abroad of considerable changes being to be made at Court, as well as among the chief men of the long robe, are again vanished ; the Lord Chancellor * and the Chief Justice† con-

---

* Jefferies.
† Sir Robert Wright. He had succeeded Sir Edward Herbert, and continued Chief Justice till after the Revolution. Roger North says of him, that " he was a creature of

tinuing as they were, and the Attorney and
Solicitor being to go the circuits, which they
would have hardly done, if greater honour than
that of a Baronet, or greater preferment than
the Solicitor already hath, had been near at
hand.

Some words are said to have passed between
the Lord Chancellor and the Master of the
Rolls,* but all matters seem to be made up
again, and all things to be left as they were.

Several others are named in the common discourse of the town, as likely to be added to
the number of the Privy Council, and most of
them are country gentlemen, such as two of
the last are, but we will spare their names till
a greater certainty.

Yesterday it was commonly reported, though

Jefferies's, and a tool that would do any thing." "A dunce
and no lawyer ; not worth a groat, having spent his estate by
debauched living ; of no truth nor honesty, but guilty of
wilful perjury to gain the borrowing of a sum of money."
See Life of Lord Keeper Guilford, and that nobleman's conversation with James respecting the character of Wright.

* Sir John Trevor.

without any grounds or reasons, for what yet appears, that the Earl of Sunderland, Lord President, in consideration of his great services done to the Crown, is to be removed from his office into a higher; but this will want time to confirm it.

Their Majesties intend to remove to Windsor about the 24th instant, at which time the Prince will be placed at Richmond, and the Princess may likely go to Tunbridge, where the fire (we have already mentioned to have happened of late) consumed about 2000*l.* worth of buildings belonging to Esq. Neill, though that doth not at all seem to diminish the company and concourse thither.

We have it from abroad, that the Elector of Bavaria, rather than the Christian cause against the Turks should longer suffer by his opiniousness and absence, hath generously offered himself to command the German army; and though there were several factions in the Emperor's Council, some for, others against it, yet there being then but little hopes of the Duke of Lor-

rain's recovery, at least of his being able to serve
this campaign, it was resolved that the Elector
of Bavaria should command in chief, and was
accordingly to set out the 5th instant at farthest.

The Duke of Lorraine's distemper is said to
be that which is very modish in another Court
and country, a fistula ; and the letters newly
arrived, revive our hopes he may escape, for
that an incision having been made, and a vast
quantity of matter issuing out, that Prince has
found great ease, and seems to be in a fair way
of recovery.

Yesterday was likely a critical day at Cologne, being the day appointed for the choosing
that Elector. The contestations are supposed
to be very sharp ; the two main weapons, of
money and self-preservation, clashing on both
sides : the Cardinal of Furstembergh wanting no French money to support his pretensions, and having the French forces to back
them ; Prince Clement of Bavaria, having
likewise his brother's purse, and all the estate

left him by the late Elector's will, to spread and spend amongst his friends, and the interest of the Empire (in opposing the French) lying on his side.

The Empress* uses all arts and interest to oppose the Cardinal, and would rather that her own brother, the Prince of Newburgh,† who is Bishop of Breslau, should succeed than any body ; yet the Pope is inclined for the Prince of Bavaria, and is said to have sent him his dispensation even before the election, which the French look upon as a piece of partiality.

The Cardinal, seeing these potent adversaries on all parts, and knowing himself to have the strongest side, yet, to make his title more plausible, hath consulted the civilians of those

* Eleanor Magdalen, daughter of Philip William Count Palatine of Newburg, married October 15th, 1676, to the Emperor Leopold, whose third wife she was. She was the mother of the Emperors Joseph I. and Charles VI. She died January 19th, 1720.

† Joseph Clement, who became eventually Elector of Cologne, and who is mentioned a few lines before as " Prince Clement of Bavaria."

countries, whether, in the interregnum of the
Electorship, he might take the Government
into his own hands : who have all answered in
the negative, for that his coadjutorship was
not confirmed by the Pope.

The Princess of Bavaria's marriage with the
Prince of Tuscany * is said to be again in danger of breaking off, upon a punctilio between
the Elector of Bavaria and the Great Duke,
who shall sign the treaty in the first place.

The opinion of the Quietists † is said to be

* Violante Beatrix, sister of Maximilian Emmanuel
Elector of Bavaria, and daughter of the Elector Ferdinand
Maria and of his wife Henrietta Adelaide of Savoy, married
in 1689 Ferdinand Hereditary Prince of Tuscany, and son of
the Grand-duke Cosmo the Third. Ferdinand died in his
father's lifetime without children, and his next brother Gas-
ton was the last Grand-duke of the House of Medicis.

† The Quietists were the followers of Madame Guyon, the
enthusiastic religionist of the time of Lewis the Fourteenth,
who, as well as her follower the virtuous Fenelon, was
cruelly persecuted for the opinions she held and propagated,
and which were called " Quietism."——" Elle prêchait le re-
noncement entière à soi-même, le silence de l'âme, l'anéantisse-
ment de toutes ses puissances, le culte intérieur, l'amour pur
et désintéressé (de Dieu), qui n'est ni avili par la crainte, ni

broke out anew in several places of France and Italy.

We hear nothing of any action yet done by the French fleet.

For John Ellis, Esq. Secretary to the
Commissioners for the Revenue of
Ireland,   At Dublin.

CXLVIII.

The Queen of Sweden at Rome.—Other Italian news.—
Marriages.

London, July 12th, 1688.

SIR,

OUR French letters would fain insinu-
ate us as if the Swedish Envoy at that Court,
having made overture in the behalf of the
King his Master,* for that Crown's renewing
its former alliance with France, and for its
being engaged to traverse the designs which

animé de l'espoir des récompenses."—Voltaire, Siècle de
Louis Quatorze.
   * Charles the Eleventh, King of Sweden, best known as
the father of the heroic Charles the Twelfth.

the new Elector of Brandenburgh may entertain in favour of the House of Austria, on
condition satisfaction be given it as to the
pensions still owing it ; several millions had
accordingly been taken out of the treasury to
that purpose ; but this piece of news coming
through so suspicious a channel, will require
great confirmation, having indeed more the
air of a French novel's policy, than of the
truth of history.

The letters from Rome confirm that the
Queen of Sweden* having had notice that a
Neapolitan, accused of enormous crimes, had
been taken up in her quarter of Franchises, she
immediately sent to the Cardinal-governor, to
require his being set at liberty, and that otherwise she would send to free him out of prison
by main force ; and the Cardinal having made

* Christina Queen of Sweden, who had abdicated the
throne of Sweden, and was now settled at Rome, where she
died April 19th, 1689. The anecdote of her in this letter is
very characteristic, and well worthy of the cruel murderess
of the unhappy Monaldeschi. She appears to have been alto-
gether one of the most hateful women that ever lived.

nswer, that in such case he should make his
complaints to the Pope; the Queen in anger
ent to fetch him that accuses the malefactor,
and detaining him prisoner in her palace, told
him that if he did not procure the prisoner to
be released in two hours' time, she would have
him thrown down out of the windows. The
Cardinal-governor fearing this might cause
some disorder in the city by the union of the
Ambassadors, thought the best expedient would
be to let out the prisoner, saying, they had mis-
taken him for another, and by this means satisfied both the Queen and the Pope.

Our Italian advices acquaint us with a tragi-
cal story, that two persons who were contract-
ed, repairing to a church in the country of Orto
to marry, the priest having asked the lady
if she accepted the person to whom she was
betrothed for her true and faithful husband,
she answered, no; which very much surprised
all the company. The priest, thinking this negative to have come from her heedlessly, reiterated his demand twice more; but the fair one

persisted in her first answer, which provoked the bridegroom to such a degree, that without respect of place or persons, he immediately stabbed his bride ; but one of her lovers being then in the church, did instantly revenge his mistress's death, for he rushed upon her murderer with his sword in his hand, and sent him to wed her in the other world. This raised such a tumult on all sides, that seven were killed, and many wounded in the church.

Our last Neapolitan letters left them still under dreadful apprehensions of the earthquake, it having been still reiterated, though above seventy thousand persons are said to have already perished.

The Lord Cornbury* is said to have been

* Edward Lord Cornbury, afterwards third Earl of Clarendon. He married Catherine O'Bryen, sole daughter of the Lord O'Bryen, eldest son of Henry sixth Earl of Thomond, by his wife Lady Catherine Stuart, sister and sole heiress of Charles last Duke of Richmond and Lennox, and also sole heiress of her mother Catherine daughter of the Lord Clifton; which barony she inherited. Henry Lord O'Bryen was one of the persons lost in the Gloucester frigate, (which was wrecked upon one of the Yarmouth sands,

married on Tuesday last to the Lady Obrian, sister and heiress to the Lord Obrian, who unhappily perished with the Glocester frigate: the Earl of Thomond giving 6000*l.* with her at present ;* and, after the decease of Sir Joseph

---

called the Lemon and Oar,) while accompanying James Duke of York to Scotland,—upon the occasion when the Duke is said to have been more anxious about saving his dogs than his friends. Lord O'Bryen's widow had remarried with Sir Joseph Williamson. The issue of Lord Cornbury's marriage was a son, Edward, who died at the age of twenty-two, unmarried, and two daughters, whereof Catherine died single, and Theodosia married John Bligh, Esq. and carried the barony of Clifton into the family of Lord Darnley.

* In the Diary of Henry Lord Clarendon is the following account of the marriage, which does not agree with what is said in this letter respecting the bride's present fortune :

" July 10th, 1688. When I came home from prayers in the morning, my wife told me my son was gone away with Mrs. O'Brian, my Lady Catherine's daughter : which struck me to the heart. The more I think of it, the more it troubles me. I had been in treaty this last year with my Lady Catherine and Sir Joseph Williamson, for this young lady, at my son's desire, for I had no kind of acquaintance with them ; but *finding she had no portion,* without which I can make no settlements, and that her estate does not come to her part till the Duke of Richmond's debts are paid, which are still near 14,000*l.* I broke very fairly off. It is the most inconvenient

Williamson's* lady, an estate of 6000*l.* *per annum,* it is said, will descend to her.

match that could have been for me; a young woman oddly bred, no manner of advantage, and an unavoidable charge. Besides, it is a base thing, and unbecoming a man of honour, to steal a child from a parent, and what no man would willingly have to be his own case. I thank God I had no hand in it. O Lord! make me able to bear this irrecoverable blow. Good God! that my poor family should be brought into utter misery by him who was the only hopes of raising it. O Lord! my heart is even broke! My brother, whose kindness is never wanting, quickly came to me, but I told him I would not see my son, nor take any notice of the match. He went then to my Lady Catherine, who was full of indignation; as I confess she had reason to be. My wife, who had always been as fond of my son as if he had been her own, helped him all she could in this match, believing it a convenient and advantageous match for him; but finding I was so much troubled at it, she took a lodging for them in Leicester Fields, whither they came in the evening. It seems they were married at Totteridge." By subsequent entries in Lord Clarendon's Diary, it appears that all parties were shortly after this reconciled to the marriage in question.

* Sir Joseph Williamson had been Secretary of State during a part of the reign of Charles the Second, and had also been employed in a diplomatic capacity. Evelyn gives by no means a flattering character of him. " Sir Joseph Williamson, Secretary of State, was son of a clergyman somewhere in Cumberland, brought up at Queen's College, of which he

On the latter end of the last week, Madam Anne Capell, the late Earl of Essex's daughter, was married to the Lord Morpeth,* but,

came to be a Fellow; then travelled with . . . . . . and returning when the King was restored, was received as a Clerk under Sir Edward Nicholas; Sir Henry Bennett (now Lord Arlington) succeeding, Williamson is transferred to him, who loving his ease more than business (though sufficiently able, had he applied himself to it,) remitted all to his man Williamson, and in a short time let him so into the secret of affairs, that (as his Lordship himself told me) there was a kind of necessity to advance him; and so by his subtlety, dexterity, and insinuation, he got now to be Principal Secretary; absolutely Lord Arlington's creature, and ungrateful enough. It has been the fate of this obliging favourite, to advance those who soon forgot their original. Sir Joseph was a musician, could play at *Jeu de Gollets*, exceeding formal, a severe master to his servants, but so inward with my Lord Obrian, that a few months after that gentleman's death he married his widow, who, being sister and heir of the Duke of Richmond, brought him a noble fortune. 'Twas thought they lived not so kindly after marriage as they did before. She was much censured for marrying so meanly, being herself allied to the Royal Family."—Diary, vol. i.—Sir Joseph died in 1701, having been a great benefactor to public endowments and charities.

* Charles (Howard) Viscount Morpeth, and on the death of his father in 1692, third Earl of Carlisle. He held at different times of his life various offices of honour and trust, and

through the greenness of their years, do not yet cohabit together.

His Majesty is said to have given order, by reason of the heat and frequency of the small-pox, that the Lady Governess permit no people to see the Prince.

The Queen's guard-chamber at Whitehall is embellished like that of the King, with arms and armour hung round the walls.

. The Lord Godolphin is said to have gone yesterday to prepare the lodgings for his Royal Highness the Prince of Wales's reception.

For John Ellis, Esq. Secretary to the
    Commissioners for the Revenue of
    Ireland,   At Dublin.

---

was the builder of the noble mansion of Castle Howard. He died January 1st, 1738 ; having married Lady Anne Capel, only surviving daughter of that illustrious and patriotic nobleman, Arthur first Earl of Essex, whose mysterious end in the Tower has caused so much comment and speculation.

CXLIX.

Interest of Philip Ellis at Court.—The Declaration.—Private matters.

Norwich, July 12th, 1688.

SIR,

IT hath been so long since I have heard from you, that I begin to fear I must lose your correspondence. I confess we are now at a great distance; however I should be loth our old friendship should be forgotten. Your brother being now a great man at Court, I have been expecting that by his interest a translation might be procured for you to some place in the English Court, as advantageous to you as that you have in the Irish; and I hope some time or other it may be done, that I may have my good friend again, where I may sometimes have the happiness of enjoying his conversation. Things look cloudy upon us here, and the matter of the Declaration hath, I fear, put us much under the King's displeasure; however, I thank God, we still live in quiet, and if God continues that, we may be content pati-

ently to bear all things else.   At present we are
only hurt in imagination, and our greatest tor-
ment is our fears of what may after happen ;
but I hope they will prove to be only fears, and
nothing else.   I hope, when you come into
England, you may think Norwich worth your
seeing, when you have a friend here that would
so heartily make you welcome.   I have now
lived here two years in great content, it being
the most delightful city of any I have seen in
England for a man to live in, especially in our
district, which hath all sorts of conveniences
to recommend it to our satisfaction.   There is
still some money due unto you from me, and it
hath lain in London for you now near these
two years, but it being the last account I am
like to make with you, I would gladly have
your full discharge when it is paid you, and
therefore I hope your occasions may ere long
call you to London, and then all things shall
be made even between us.   I confess I am the
more cautious, because the last 15*l.* paid you
had like to have been lost through the death of

your kinsman, to whom it was to be paid, and I only owe it to Mr. Pitt's negligence in omitting to give him the bill when he ought, that it was not. Pray favour me to let me hear from you when you have leisure, and you will very much oblige,

Sir,

Your most affectionate and faithful

Humble servant,

HUMPHRY PRIDEAUX.*

For John Ellis, Esq. Secretary to
the Treasury in

Dublin.

---

* This letter was written by the learned and pious Humphrey Prideaux, the Author of many works of Divinity, and especially of the admirable " Connexion of the History of the Old and New Testament," which has caused his name to be known and revered even in our own times. At the time he wrote this letter he was settled at Norwich, of which cathedral he was a prebendary, having left Oxford, where he had previously resided, in consequence of James's imposing a Roman Catholic dean upon Christ-church. In the end of this year he was made Archdeacon of Norwich, and in 1702 became Dean of the same place. He closed his long and useful life on the 1st of November, 1724, at the age of seventy-six.

CI.

Election at Cologne. — Ecclesiastical Commission. — Fire-works on the Thames.—Blessed clouts sent by the Pope.

London, July 17th, 1688.

SIR,

On Friday last, as we have already mentioned, we had the news of the late election at Cologne, how that Prince Clement of Bavaria was chosen Elector of that diocese, notwithstanding all the intrigues and opposition of Cardinal Furstembergh. The news came by express to Bruxelles just as the post for England came away, so that we have not yet the particulars: we may so far guess at them as to assure ourselves great endeavours were used on both sides, and whatever interest the one made, that the other still countermined it; and as the French seldom failed before in their game, so it is clear when others use the same charms with themselves, they may conquer. It was likely a false step in the Cardinal in not putting some French troops in the city, which would have much influenced his party, but as that would likely have intimidated the electors, in appearance at least, so, for aught we know, the Cardinal may yet protest against this election for several reasons; as first, for that large offers of money are said to have been made underhand by the partizans of Prince Clement, which will with little rigour of law be expounded to squint towards what some call simony; secondly, the Pope will be protested against for seeming to act so partially in favour of Prince Clement, being said to have granted dispensations to the Prince before he was elected. One ill consequence of this election may happen to be a dispute about the evacuations of those places into which some of the Cardinal's troops are entered, of which time must give us an account.

The discourse here at present is what will be the end of the order of the Lords for Ecclesiastical Causes, whereby all Archdeacons and Chancellors are required to send the names of such clergymen in their dioceses as have and have not read the Declaration.

Sir John Narborough is said to have been taken ill of a fever, and to be dead ; but this will want confirmation.

My Lord Mordant * is said to be arrived. This evening the fireworks upon the Thames will be played : the devices of them are very ingenious, and too long to be here inserted. There are several thousands of balloons that are to be shot into the air, and then to fall into the river, and represent several figures.   There are twelve mortar-pieces, that are to cast granado shells into the air, which, when they break, will discover odd mixtures and shapes.   The figure of Bacchus represents Plenty, out of whose great tun and belly are to be discharged about eight or nine barrels of combustibles. There are also two large female figures, which represent Fecundity and Loyalty; the emblems of the first are a hare and a hen and chickens, each of which are, in their proper time, to act their part in the magnificent show of this evening.

* Afterwards the celebrated Earl of Peterborough.   He had been with the Prince of Orange in Holland.

Letters newly arrived from Flanders confirm
to us the election of Prince Clement of Bavaria,
but we have not time to insert farther particulars, than that the first thing the Chapter did
was unanimously to agree that he that should
be chosen Archbishop and Elector, should not
take possession of the Regency before such
time that he had his confirmation from the
Pope. These advices add, that the Bishop of
Breslaw was gone for Munster, with a fair
prospect of obtaining the prelacy.

Our Italian letters continue to speak of the
dismal confusion occasioned by the late earth-
quakes: that they had now again taken out 400
persons alive from under the ruins of the houses,
and among others a lady with child, who,
through a kind of miracle, had there continued
buried, though alive, for eleven days together,
even without drinking or eating. And that a
pillar of fire had been seen to fly in the air over
the city of Coritto.

At the same time, they tell us of the extraordinary joy at Rome upon the birth of the

Prince of Wales, and that it was expected
his Holiness would suddenly nominate M. Bar-
berino, or some other prelate, to carry his
Royal Highness the blessed clouts.

For John Ellis, Esq. Secretary to the
    Commissioners for the Revenue of
    Ireland,

                    at Dublin.

CLI.

Removal of the Court.—Prince of Wales's petition respect-
    ing Hackney-coaches and Foundlings.—Reports.—Foreign
    news, &c.

                        London, July 19th, 1688.

SIR,

    ORDERS are given for carriage and
other necessaries for the removal of the Court,
to be ready next Monday; and on Tuesday
their Majesties depart for Windsor, the Prince
to Richmond, and the Princess of Denmark to
Tunbridge.

It is yet uncertain whether the King designs
a progress this summer; if so, it will likely be

towards York. But the Scots would have it somewhat farther.

The Lady Marquess of Powis, governante to the Prince, hath taught his Royal Highness a way to ask already : for, few days ago, his Royal Highness was brought to the King with a petition in his hand, desiring that 200 hackney-coaches may be added to the 400 now licensed, but that the revenue for that said 200 might be applied towards the feeding and breeding of foundling children.

The Judges * were introduced to the King last Sunday by the Lord Chancellor, and had their charge and instructions given them before they go their circuits. It is said they are to repeat the same assurances to the Counties, that his Majesty is resolved to convene a Parliament in November, and to direct that such members be chosen as will comply with his

* "June 13th, 1688.—In the afternoon I was with my Lord Chancellor. As for the Judges, said he, they are most of them rogues."—" Aug. 13th, 1688.—I was at Bulstrode. Lord Chancellor talked to me very freely of all affairs, called the Judges a thousand fools and knaves."—Entries in Lord Clarendon's Diary.

Majesty's intentions, which are for the ease and quiet of his subjects.

What is said of the Prince of Orange having sent five Dutch men of war, and their having made a descent upon St. Christopher's, and driven the French thence, and seized the place by way of reprisals for what the French did at Orange, is very uncertain, and is an invention of those that love to feed the town with the air of novels.

Mr. Harcott, a Justice of Peace of Islington, was one of the jury which acquitted the Bishops. He did a little before, or after that time, promise to give his consent and interest for repealing the penal laws and tests ; but last sessions at Hicks's Hall, he made a formal motion and desired to be heard, saying, that he was heartily sorry and penitent for what he was tempted to do against his conscience, in promising to repeal the laws of the land, and he utterly recanted and retracted what he had before said and done. He is a man of a reddish complexion, and was ever fickle in his resolutions.

As to the election of Cologne, we have these farther particulars : that the Cardinal had 13 votes, and Prince Clement but 10, yet the last had the Pope's bull and dispensation ; and which soever had it not, must have had two-thirds of the votes on his side, which are in all 23 in the whole chapter. Besides that, if the Cardinal had had two-thirds and a dispensation, yet he could never have been a complete Elector, for the Emperor will never consent to give him investiture, which is essential to all members of the Empire. So that Prince Clement, having the Emperor, the Pope, and all Germany, as well as the laws, on his side, will no doubt be declared Elector, and nothing but the French *cannon-law* can hinder it. In the mean time, the Cardinal is putting his French troops into the towns and garrisons, and we may in time hear how this dealing of the Pope will be resented by the French King.

Fresh propositions of peace were sent to the Emperor from the Turks : how far this will be relished we may know in few days.

Two thousand bombs are thrown into Algiers, but without any great success, which the Algierines have answered by shooting into the fleet the French Consul's head.

An eagle is said to have been seen flying over the city of Paris, to the great astonishment of the beholders, and that he perched upon or near the statue of the French King, set up in Place Saint Victoire,* where the people, luring of him with meat, drew him down and caught him, and being a foreign bird, may be in danger of the Bastile.

The *mobile* at Amsterdam did, at the English Consul's celebrating the birth of the Prince of Wales, commit such rudenesses as require severe resentment.

For John Ellis, Esq. Secretary to the
 Commissioners for the Revenue of
 Ireland,   at Dublin.

---

* This was the pedestrian statue of Lewis the Fourteenth, set up in the Place des Victoires at Paris by the Marshal De la Feuillade at his own expense, and at the feet of which, by a refinement of flattery rarely equalled, the Marshal intended to be buried. For this purpose, he had contrived a subterraneous passage under the *Place*, which ended in a vault constructed exactly under the statue.

CLII.

Prince of Wales's establishment.—Lord Chancellor's son
married.—Chief Justice Herbert.—Clerical news, &c.

London, July 21st, 1688.

SIR,

An establishment of the Prince of
Wales's household is made, wherein Sir Ste-
phen Fox is said to have had a hand, and in
most places to have put those that are or were
his own servants and relations.

On Tuesday last was solemnized the marriage of my Lord Chancellor's son* with the
daughter of the late Earl of Pembroke,† in

---

* John Jefferies, afterwards the second and last Lord Jefferies. He died in 1703. There is a strange story told of this
Lord with regard to Dryden's funeral, in Wilson's Memoirs of
Congreve; but which appears, from Mr. Malone's researches,
to have been exceedingly incorrectly related, if not entirely a
falsehood. It may be found in all accounts of the life of
Dryden.

† Philip (Herbert) seventh Earl of Pembroke, married
Henrietta de Querouaille, youngest sister of the Duchess of
Portsmouth, and died August 29th, 1683. The sole issue of
this marriage was a daughter, Charlotte, married to John

favour of whom against the present Earl a decree passed in Chancery this last term : her mother, who is the Duchess of Portsmouth's sister, was present at the marriage, and though she be a Roman Catholic, yet consented the marriage should be performed by a Protestant minister. This match affords matter of discourse.

A patent is passing for Lord Chief Justice Herbert of the manor of Oatlands,* one of the

second Lord Jefferies, by whom she became the mother of an only daughter, Henrietta Louisa, afterwards married to Thomas Earl of Pomfret. Lord Jefferies died May 9th, 1703, and his widow remarried with Thomas Viscount Windsor in Ireland, Baron Mountjoy in England.

* The manor of Oatlands in Surrey had belonged to the Crown from the time of Henry the Eighth. On the Restoration it was given to the Queen Dowager, Henrietta Maria, who granted a beneficial lease of it to her supposed lover, Jermyn, Earl of St. Albans. In 1688, Sir Edward Herbert purchased the lease of Lord St. Albans. Upon this, James, to reward Sir Edward for his compliances with the wishes of the Court, granted to the Chief Justice an additional lease of seventy-six years. As Sir Edward followed the fortunes of James on his abdication, his interest in the manor of Oatlands became forfeited, and was granted by William III. to his

King's palaces, where his Lordship is building of a house, though Mr. Daniel Sheldon hath a lease and term of years in the place, and was the person that first introduced his Lordship into the air and knowledge of the said place. His Lordship in his charge to the Jury at Aylesbury said, the King will call a Parliament in November at farthest, and recommended to them the choice of such members as would comply with the King in repealing the penal laws and the Tests.

The Bishops that were lately in the Tower, are gone to their respective Bishopricks, and have resolved to hold frequent catechisings and confirmations ; and last week the Archbishop began at Lambeth, and at Croydon, in Surry, where the Bishop of Gloucester assisted him in confirming several thousands of children, that were brought to them.

This good example is followed also by the

brother, Arthur Herbert, the Admiral, whom he also created Earl of Torrington. In 1696, William granted the fee simple of this manor to the said Earl.

Roman Clergy about the town ; and last week, Bishop Ellis, assisted by Father Poulton the Jesuit, confirmed some hundreds of youth (some of them were new converts) at the New Chapel in the Savoy.

Sir John Narborough is confidently reported to have died on the 27th of May,* and the loss of him much regretted, not only by those concerned with him in the silver fishing, but by all that knew him to be an honest man, an able seaman, and an useful subject. Some will have the advice of his death not to be positive ; others again just now assure me, that a ship is newly arrived with his body.

The Bishop of Durham † is still indisposed, and has suspended several of his clergy, particularly Dr. Morton, his chaplain, for not reading the Declaration. The Bishop of Chester ‡ is said to intend the same thing in his diocese,

* This report turned out to be true. King James forthwith created his eldest son John a Baronet, as an acknowledgment of his father's merits.

† Crewe, Bishop of Durham.

‡ Cartwright, Bishop of Chester.

and especially at Chester, where the Dean is affirmed to have once promised the reading, and then to have lien sick a-bed when the day came, so that it was not read in the Cathedral.

His Majesty returned yesterday at noon from the Buoy in the Nore, where he spent a whole day in viewing his squadron of ships, and is said to have given orders for the equiping of ten more.

The Archbishop and the Clergy of London are said to have had several conferences with the chief of the Dissenting ministers, in order to agree such points of ceremonies as are indifferent between them, and to take their measures for what is to be proposed about religion at next Parliament.

Our foreign news is inconsiderable; only that the Germans still pick up the remaining places in Hungary. The Turks are said to have abandoned Illock and Peterwaradin, stealing away in the night.

The Emperor's council begin to think of peace, and the major part are averred to be for

it, and some are for the war, and these are such
as find their interest in it.   The demolishing of
Belgrade is said to be one point the Emperor
would have, and the Turks will hardly grant.

For John Ellis, Esq. Secretary to the
Commissioners for the Revenue of
Ireland at Dublin.

Dublin.

CLIII.

Turkish news.—Death of the Duke of Ormonde.—Rumours
from France.—Duke of Albemarle.

London, July 24th, 1688.

SIR,

WE cannot hear that the French fleet
have taken right measures in making up their
bombs, which do but little execution there
this campaign ; the Turks seeming to slight
their fury, with which they are now so well
acquainted.

Some letters by way of France say, that a
new flame of confusion is broke out in Turkey,

and that, as it is thought, by the instigation of Yeghen Bassa, who, to be revenged on the Grand Seignior and his Ministers for declaring him rebel, hath corrupted most of the Bassas in Europe, and drawn them on his side to declare for a free government, which they intend to devise and canton among themselves; and the scheme is said to be so deeply laid, that the Sultan thought of scampering into Asia, but this may seem too considerable to be true; but if the heads of the army once combine, this and more may be brought about, besides that some of them may be better contented to pursue the war and their own interest, than be laid aside and lose the sweet opportunity of plunder by a peace.

On Friday last died the greatest man and best of subjects, the Duke of Ormond, who hath had the honour to outdo all the subjects in Europe, by his gallant actions and constant loyalty and integrity to his Prince for above fifty years together. He died in Dorsetshire, but, it is thought, will be buried in Westminster

Abbey. His Garter will likely be given to the Duke of Barwick, and his place of Lord Steward of the Household * to the Marquis of Powis, though it be not yet declared.

The French King is said to be inviting back his subjects from all parts, especially the handi-craft part of them, whose departure is said to have much prejudiced his revenue, and pro-miseth them his toleration; though it doth not appear they are forward to believe that an or-der of Council can preserve what the Edict of Nantes could not.

The French give out they will meddle no more in the matters of Cologne, but suffer it to take its fate; if so, the French troops will be recalled, and the Cardinal must pack away to his own Bishopric of Strasburgh, which, with his life, he owes to France. We may very soon hear what the success will be at Liege and Munster.

* It does not appear that any Lord Steward of the House-hold was appointed till after the Revolution, when William gave the place to Lord Devonshire.

Amongst other competitors for Mr. Sheridan's place, are named Mr. Hales, Mr. Knightly, and Mr. Trinder. Mr. Dickenson, one of the Commissioners in Ireland, would have excused his going back into that kingdom, but we hear that his Majesty thought fit to overrule him.

What is reported of the Duke of Albemarle's death, we hope, is a mistake. The heart of Sir John Narborough is brought over and delivered to his relations: his widow is said to be worth 80,000*l.* Mr. Wm. Constable, who was supercargo on board him, is also arrived, and says there are not above 1200*l.* fished up this last expedition; that about 500,000*l.* have been taken up in all; that there is much more behind, and that they have left a guard there upon the wreck, in order to begin betimes next season.

The church of Wrexham, in Wales, was lately robbed, and all the plate and linen taken away.

The King and Queen move to Windsor this

day, and the Princess to Tunbridge.   The
Prince of Wales goes on Friday to Richmond:
the issue made in his shoulder is dried up by
the advice of chirurgeons.

A whale of vast bulk being said to be ham-
pered in a creek near Malden, in Essex, doth
occasion great resort thither.

For John Ellis, Esq. Secretary to the
    Commissioners for the Revenue of
    Ireland,
                    At Dublin.

CLIV.

**The Court at Windsor.—Affairs of Cologne.—A Priest
insulted, &c.**

London, July 26th, 1688.

SIR,

On Tuesday, their Majesties went for
Windsor, and to-morrow the Prince of Wales
is to remove for Richmond.   His Royal Highness goes abroad in the Park every day to take
the air.

What our last told you of the new disorders at Constantinople, seems to be confirmed from all parts. The rabble are drawn in to join with the mutinous part of the army, and all seem to despise the Grand Signior ; so far, that he cannot think himself safe where he is, and so meditateth a retreat into Asia. The plague is said to be increased also, which adds to the misery and despair of that Government.

The most Christian King is said to have writ a civil letter to the Pope in behalf of Cardinal Furstemberg, to demand his justice, for much favour cannot be expected in his case ; and that King begins to lay to the Pope's charge any war or misery that shall befall Christendom upon the account of that election. In the mean time the new electors protest against each other ; and some would be glad of a composition in the matter, and please both, by giving the Electorship to the Cardinal, and the Coadjutorship to the Prince of Bavaria.

Algiers begins now to be sensible of the French bombs, the best part of their town being beaten down and reduced to ruins; yet the Turks bear it with great vigour and resolution, and continue to shoot off Frenchmen in return of their bombs.

Colonel Molesworth* is returned from Jamaica, together with Mr. Constable. The Duke of Albemarle hath sent complaints against the first; but he hopes to justify himself, and to lay the fault elsewhere.

Six thousand Piedmontese are said to have got together in arms, and to have cut the throats of most of those officers and soldiers that were posted in their countries by the Duke of Savoy's command.

The French Court hath lately created a new tribunal, to inquire into the bribery and corruption of their judges.

* Hender Molesworth, Esq. created a Baronet by King William in 1689. He had been President of the island of Jamaica during the reign of Charles the Second, and subsequently Lieutenant-governor of the same, till the arrival of the Duke of Albemarle. Upon the death of the Duke of Albemarle there in the beginning of 1689, he was constituted Governor of the Island.

What is said by some newsmongers about the town, of four soldiers having shot at Father Peters in the camp, is false, no such indignity having been offered to any of the fathers; only one of the King's priests happened to be riding by, eight miles from the camp, as two soldiers were a-drinking the King's health, and out of gaiety discharged their muskets; and this was found to be the fact upon examination at a Council of War.

We have every month some new relation from the East Indies. Now they tell us, how the great Mogul hath beheaded the King of Golconda, and lately how the English had beat the Mogul. But all these tidings may possibly be interpreted some of the shams and amusements of a body of men trading into those parts; they may well seem to require better authority.

For John Ellis, Esq. Secretary to the
   Commissioners for the Revenue of
   Ireland,   At Dublin.

CLV.

New Bishop of Oxford, &c.

28th July, 1688.

SIR,

MR. Trinder, who is made one of your Commissioners, is a very fair-conditioned gentleman: his zeal in his way will be no part of his business at your Board.

One Mr. Hall,* Rector of Allhallows Stayning, always a moderate man, and now particularly meritorious for having read the Declaration, is made Bishop of Oxon. Other removes in the Church from Chester to York, &c. are talked of, but spread about by those that wish them.

The Prince removed yesterday to Richmond.

* Timothy Hall, Bishop of Oxford. Besides his living of Allhallows, he was also Rector of Horsington in Buckinghamshire. Burnet gives the following account of his elevation: —" One Hall, a Conformist in London, who was looked on as half a Presbyterian, yet, because he read the Declaration, was made Bishop of Oxford." He succeeded Parker, who was just dead.

All here quiet, barren of all news and ordinary conversation. I hope Spence tells you more.

Pray send me a copy of the order for stopping of lambskins: I shall only use the *date of it*.

(No address on this letter.)

CLVI.

Foreign news.—Changes in the Church.—Dukes of Ormonde.
—Duchess of Portsmouth gone to France.

London, July 28th, 1688.

SIR,

WE hear no farther account from Cologne, all parties seeming to acquiesce with great resignation till the Pope shall give his decision in the case, either by confirming the postulation of the Cardinal, or the election of Prince Clement. In the mean time, as nothing is more uneasy to the Cardinal than to be quiet, so he is marching and cross-marching his troops about the Electorate, that he may not be unprovided, in case the point cannot be decided without blows.

One Prebeck, prebend of that church, is chosen Bishop of Hildesheime, and is a person so beloved in his neighbourhood, that he may go near to be put up for some other of the new vacant bishopricks.

The Imperial Army is said to be entered into Sclavonia, and thence they seem resolved to pass over the Save, and to go and attack Belgrade, where some report all to be in a disorderly condition, and scarce an enemy will be found. Others think that the Turks would decoy the Germans over the river, and then spend what vigour they have in cutting off their retreat; so that many wish the Emperor may not too late repent the desire of extending his dominions beyond what was once hoped for, and beyond those bounds which they fancy God and Nature seem to have given to his Empire.

We do not find that Yeghen Pacha has yet

made his peace, since the confusions are said to be broke out anew at Constantinople, and that by his instigation ; and on this side he and the Pacha of Belgrade exercise their cruelties, by reprisals upon each other's adherents, the one having lately sent a compliment to the other with a hundred heads of his friends, which the other returned in the like bloody number and manner.

Great disputes there are at Vienna, whether Monsieur de Villars,* the French Ambassador, ought to be suffered to follow the Duke of Bavaria into the field, or no, most being against it.

The Elector of Brandeburgh has refused to renew his treaties with the States-General till they give him some satisfaction for two places

---

* Lewis Claude Duke de Villars, one of the most conspicuous of the generals of Lewis the Fourteenth. He possessed considerable talents, and at least an equal share of vanity and *fanfaronade.* He was made a Marshal in 1702, and President of the Council of War in 1718. He died in 1734.

or forts which they detain from him in Africa upon the coast of Guinea.

One Mr. Hall, Rector of Allhallows in the city of London, being one of the clergymen that read the Declaration, and said to be most deserving of the four, is made Bishop of Oxford, and the *Congé d'élire* is gone down.

We talk of other changes in the Church, as if the Bishop of Chester were to be translated to the Archbishopric of York, and his Dean to succeed him, but this is not declared.

Sir Humphrey Edwynne, late Treasurer of the East India Company, and one Johnson of Mile-end Green, are named to succeed as Sheriffs of the City of London for the next year.

We are told the University of Oxford have elected the young Duke of Ormond* to be their Chancellor, but that his Grace is not willing to accept of it, since his Majesty had recommended another of eminent place and qua-

---

* James second Duke of Ormonde. The University abided by its choice, and the Duke eventually became the Chancellor of it.

lity, viz. the Lord Chancellor. The Convocation was divided in their choice, for some were for the Lord Halifax, and others for the Earl of Nottingham,* and a third party for the Earl of Abingdon.†

* Daniel (Finch) second Earl of Nottingham, and towards the latter end of his life, sixth Earl of Winchilsea. He played a considerable part in the political history of this country, and was at different times of his life Secretary of State, President of the Council, and one of the Lords Justices for administering the affairs of the kingdom on the accession of George the First, and till that monarch's arrival in England. " The Earl of Nottingham had great credit with the whole church party, for he was a man possessed with their notions, and was grave and virtuous in the course of his life. He had some knowledge of the law, and of the records of Parliament, and was a copious speaker, but too florid and tedious." The tediousness and gravity of his harangues, united with a dark and rueful countenance, had obtained for him, among his contemporaries, the appellation of " *Old Dismal.*" He died January 1st, 1730.

† James (Bertie) Lord Norreys of Rycote, created Earl of Abingdon in 1682. This nobleman was one of those persons who concurred heartily in the Revolution, till it was found to be the intention that the Prince of Orange should be declared King, which their conscientious scruples obliged them to oppose. He died in 1699, leaving behind him a family consisting of six sons and three daughters.

The Duke of Ormond died, they say, upon the same day with the Duchess,* and foretold he himself should die that day, and has cautioned the young Duke to have a care of it likewise.

We do not hear his Majesty does this year intend any progress either Northward or Westward, otherwise than to Portsmouth.

Last night the Duchess of Portsmouth went down the River, in order to embark for France.

For John Ellis, Esq. Secretary to the
    Commissioners for the Revenue of
    Ireland,
                    At Dublin.

---

* Lady Elizabeth Preston, only child of Preston Earl of Desmond, married to the Duke of Ormonde, then Lord Thurles, in 1629.   By this marriage the Duke became again possessed of his paternal estate, which had been wrested from the family by an unjust decision of James the First, in favour of his favourite, Lord Desmond.   The Duchess of Ormonde died *July* 21st, 1684; the Duke, *July* 21st, 1688.

CLVII.

Duke of Ormonde.—Prince of Wales ill and weakly.

London, July 31st, 1688.

DEAR SIR,

YOURS of the 20th I had yesterday. I had had a long ramble then, and since another, but much shorter, for I returned but on Sunday night from Cassiobury, my Lady Essex's,* where I spend much of my idle time since my Lord Morpeth (Earl Carlisle's son) married her thirteen years old daughter, the Lady Ann. He goes to travel shortly, and if I can settle matters so as to be able to go with him, I will, for clouds rise here thick, and hopes grow less and less of preferment for those that will not leap the hedge as well as the ditch.

Our young Duke of Ormonde, with his brother the Marquis of Wo'ster,† went towards

* Elizabeth (Percy) daughter of Algernon Earl of Northumberland. She was at this time the widow of Arthur first Earl of Essex.

† Charles (Somerset) Marquis of Worcester, brother-in-law of the second Duke of Ormonde.

Kingston-hall this morning, and thence design for Badminton, and yet return hither by Saturday.   I reckon you will have the particulars of the good old gentleman's end ; that it would prove a superfluous work for me to go about. He was sensible to the last, but I think, though he did not expect to live the day out, yet when death came upon him, he rather thought it was sleep, for he bade La-roche turn him, saying he was drowsy, and instantly died.   He made the young Duke sole executor, and hath left little from him. He hath the Chancellorship of Oxon. by election, which the King seems to be well content with, because they chose him ; for otherwise he would have pulled a crow with them for not acquainting him before they proceeded to election, as was customary.   The mandamus went for Lord Chancellor to be their's, but came two hours too late.*   The King

---

* Upon this occasion the Vice-Chancellor (Gilbert Ironside, Warden of Wadham College,) wrote the following base and servile letter to the infamous Jefferies :—

" My Lord,—I take this University, specially myself, to

received the young Duke kindly, took the George and put it in his pocket.   The world

be at this time extremely unhappy in reference to his Majesty and your Lordship.   His Majesty's displeasure, next to that of God's, I am sure this loyal University knows it to be their duty never to do any thing to deserve ; and will be always very careful of any neglect to your Lordship, of whose good-will and favour to us we have had so much experience."

" My Lord, his Majesty expressed a fatherly care to us in recommending your Lordship to be our Chancellor,† and your Lordship was the most desirable person in the world.   But as we had no notice of your Lordship's inclinations, or that you would accept of that office ; so, on the other hand, my late Lord Duke of Ormond's obligations to this place were so many and so great, and our presumptions that his son would stand up in his father's room were so reasonable, that the consideration of it made a speedy way for the election of his Lordship.   As for the suddenness of our election, on Sunday, at two o'clock, I had an express of my Lord Duke's death, and I am peremptorily commanded by our statutes to proceed to a new election *quam primum commode fieri poterit :* accordingly I called a Convocation on Monday morning, in which my Lord Duke that now is, was chosen by one hundred and eighty voices.   His Majesty's mandate did not come to me till yesterday in the afternoon."

" I humbly beseech your Lordship to take this true ac-

---

† This recommendation came in the form of a mandate signed by Lord Middleton as Secretary of State, directing the University to elect Jefferies their Chancellor.

says the Duke of Berwick will have it; but I am confident it is to be a sort of rod over the young gentleman's head, and his merit in next Parliament shall get or lose it. The camp breaks up in a few days, in order to get to their winter quarters before the writs come out, which I think will be speedily; and the King designs a session in November, but I think some of the Ministers are not of his mind. The representation of our friend the Lord is false. My Prior will not hold it, for he is in a deep consumption. I know not where to shift my hand, for there is no pleading without counsel in any court. I have my eye upon one that has a towardly good will for me, and I hope he may make up in assurance, what he comes short of the other in understanding. The young Prince lives on, but is a weakly

account of our affairs as an excuse for us, and according to the great goodness of your nature and good-will to this place, to offer it to his Majesty; to whose service, notwithstanding any sinister suggestions to the contrary, we are, and will be always entirely devoted. I am, &c."

" For my Lord Chancellor of England."

nfant, at Richmond. P. and Pss. of Denmark
at Tunbridge. If the Queen go to the Bath, it
will be the latter end of next month ; and the
King's progresses will be but to Portsmouth,
or such a step. We talk of a Dictator's power
given to the Prince of Orange in Holland for
a year. I cannot compass what you desire
to-night. My service to our friend Mr. H.
Temple.

Yours, J. F.

Mr. Gascoigne is Secretary to the present
Duke. What servants he wants, he will take
from his grandfather's family. I think J.
Clarke will not be of the number.

Trinder, an active Justice of Peace here, is
likeliest to succeed Mr. Sheridan in your Commission. I wish the Bishop* would spur up
for you. I will move again, as I always do,
when I see him.

It is thought Bishop Chester will be Archbishop York ;† Ardern, Dean of Chester, Bi-

* Philip Ellis.
† Lamplugh was made Archbishop of York.

shop there; and Lord Powis have the Lord Stewardship of King's Household.

The titular honour of Steward of Westminster, Winchester, and Charter-house, I think will fall to the young Duke's* share.

For John Ellis, Esq. Secretary of His
  Majesty's Revenue in Ireland.
Ireland.   At Dublin.

CLVIII.

**Promotions and Appointments.—Movements of the Court.—
Foreign news of various kinds.**

London, July 31st, 1688.

SIR,

THE instruments of making Mr. Hall Bishop of Oxford, are passing the Seals, but there is no Declaration of the King's pleasure yet come about removing the Bishop of Chester to York, which he, no doubt, endeavoured all he can for; that thereby his Dean would be made Bishop, to make room for his son to be

* Of Ormonde.

Dean, who is lately married with the bastard daughter of a certain Peer.*

We do not hear that the state of the Lord Steward of his Majesty's Household is yet given to any body. The Lord Powis and Dover are much talked of. The Dean and Chapter of Westminster have chosen the Duke of Ormond for their Lord High Steward; he had eight voices in twelve: others were put up in nomination, of high quality, as Lord Chancellor, Lord President,† Lord Chamberlain,‡ &c.

That the Queen will go to the Bath this summer, and the King upon a progress to the North, seems to be no more talked of. The Queen Dowager§ begins to be weary of the town, and would have a good country-house to pass some part of the summer in; her Majesty is said to have a mind to go to Chatsworth, the Earl of Devon's, or else will lay out a sum to build her one of her own.

* I cannot discover, nor is it of much importance, what Peer's natural daughter married Bishop Cartwright's son.
† Lord Sunderland.   ‡ Lord Mulgrave.
§ Catherine of Portugal.

Some days ago, as his Majesty was drawing out all the horse now encamped, a certain person unknown (as yet) rode up to his Majesty, letting him know he had something to say of great moment, and the King making towards him, the gentleman lighted off his horse, and being booted, fell down and broke his leg.

Here is now a discourse, that the Train Bands will be put up again, and that the Lieutenancy is already appointed.

The Duchess of Mazarine, the Duchess of Bouillon, her sister, and the Duchess of Cleveland, went down the River on board an East Indiaman, and were, it seems, so well satisfied with their fare and entertainment, that their Graces stayed two or three days.*

There is a good prospect of a happy campaign for the Christians; the Emperor had had several good hits already, and not one of the least is the meeting with several waggons of

* This seems, from the length of its duration, to have been rather a singular expedition, though not the least out of character for the heroines who undertook it.

money, most in French louis-d'ors, which was pretended to be designed to the French Ambassador in Poland, though others think they were for Count Tekely, since gold is the only guard and safety now left him.

The Prince of Poland * was led on so far by his love as to pass some days incognito at Berlin, where he had frequent views of the Princess Radzivil.†   He was observed to be conver-

---

* This was the Prince James Lewis Sobieski, eldest son of the heroic John Sobieski, King of Poland.   There is frequent mention of him made in the letters of John Sobieski to his wife Mary de la Grange d'Arquien, written during the celebrated campaign of Vienna in 1683.   In that correspondence he is called " Fanfan," a name of endearment.   He appears to have been a man of great bravery, but without much talent.   He was born at Paris, Nov. 2d, 1667, and died December 19th, 1734, and with him extinguished the male line of this illustrious family.   One of his daughters, Maria Clementina, was the wife of the *Old Pretender*.

† At the age of twenty, James Lewis was upon the point of marrying a Princess of Radzivil, the widow of a Prince of Brandenburg.   All was prepared for this union ; the young Sobieski set off for Berlin in order to conclude it ; but the Princess was already secretly married to a Prince of Neuburg.   The King of Poland, irritated with this affront, demanded a public and signal reparation from the Elector of

sant with some Frenchmen, and being not known till he was gone, the French Secretary and a French colonel were commanded by the Elector to depart his dominions in twenty-four hours.

One Plettenburg, the Dean, being chosen Bishop of Munster, it will be a disappointment to the Empress, who stickled hard for the Bishop of Breslaw, her brother.

We hear from Genoa, that all the Ecclesiastics exhort to penitence, from an old prophecy that foretells they were to expect the same fate with Naples. The ladies are already stript of all their silks and vanities by orders, and persuaded to do acts of mortification barefooted; and their very cast clothes will, they say, amount to a considerable revenue.

Brandenburgh; but all these threats ended in vain words. It was even at length agreed that James Sobieski should marry the sister of his rival, which event took place at Warsaw in 1691. "He became allied by this union to the first Catholic reigning families; the sisters of the Princess of Neuburg being married to the Emperor, the Kings of Portugal and Spain, and the Duke of Parma."—Biographie Universelle.

We expect to hear that the German army is approached to Belgrade : it is yet uncertain what the condition of that place is, and whether the Yeghen Pacha be there. He had gone near to revolt, if the Grand Vizier had not smoothed him up. Yet nothing can bear up the courage of the Turks in general, who have also got an old prophecy by the end, that about this time the Turkish Empire must be ruined by the Franks, which name they called the European Christians by : and that makes each Pacha and each Bey willing to secure what he hath, and to get what he can, so that the Turkish army seemed rather inclined to pillage and to plunder than to fight.

The Elector of Bavaria went on the 10th to the army, and the Duke of Lorrain is so well that he intends to follow him.

The Germans had the good luck to intercept a convoy, going to Great Waradin, of 800 oxen and 4000 sheep, which will further the surrendry of that place. The Prince of Walachia hath also at last shaken off his dependence upon the Turks, and given himself over to the Emperor, and is to pay 100,000 crowns yearly, and is to have his male children to succeed him, and to be provided for in the peace as one of the other Allies.

For John Ellis, Esq. Secretary to the
   Commissioners for the Revenue of
   Ireland,   At Dublin.

CLIX.

Details respecting the Death of the Duke of Ormonde.

Kingston Hall, 31st July, 1688.

SIR,

BEING here to pay my last respects to the hearse of so great a patron, and knowing the concern you will have herein, I cannot but in a few words tell you what has passed. His Grace went out on Wednesday the 18th for half a dozen miles with my Lady Ossory in the coach, but returned ill. However, he was the two next days a little about the house, till on Friday evening he was taken with a stitch : the doctor came next morning to do what he could ; but when Mr. Clarke entered the room before him, my Lord said, " James, this day four years was a sad day for me by the loss of my wife." After this, being at some ease with the stitch, he talked of all indifferent things, and took pleasure to see the child play before him. He got up at ten. Morning prayers of the family, and the same at three in the afternoon, when he answered clear and as loud as he was wont, and he joked pleasantly at sitting up, that his legs were more easy and plying than since his first illness, which yet doubtless was no other than the creeping up of the humour unto the vital parts. While he was at prayers he showed tokens in his face of being in pain, though he would not groan or complain. He appointed his chaplain to have the sacrament ready for him next morning at ten of the clock, and said that such and such should receive it with him. But desiring to go back to his bed for some refreshment, James

Clarke, observing that he declined apace, came to him at four, and asked if his Grace would please to receive the sacrament now. He answered quick and cheerfully, " Ay, with all my heart." So the Earl of Ossory with his lady and others joined with him therein, and his Grace took it with exemplary devotion. In half an hour after, he called to be turned on his side to try if he could go to rest ; but when the servant came, he found him dying, and in six minutes, without a groan or the least struggling, he was dead. In this he had his constant wish of not outliving his intellectuals.

In April last he made a short will, appointing his grandson executor ; he gave a few legacies to some servants, and appointed to be buried with his wife and two sons, and as privately as she was.

This is the short of what we now talk of. His present Grace went on Monday last to wait on the King, and is not yet returned. By Saturday we think the body will be in the grave. My Lady will go directly hence to Badminton, and thither I attend her, and so home, being always,

Sir,

Your most affectionate friend

and humble servant,

ROBERT SOUTHWELL.

Mr. John Ellis.

CLX.

Turkish news.—Various rumours.—Duke of Albemarle.

London, Aug. 2d, 1688.

SIR,

LETTERS from Constantinople of the 10th of June import that the plague there is much augmented; and that it not only very much incommoded that great city, but also that of Pera, and other neighbouring places; that the Christians withdrew thence, and though the religion of the Turks do obstinately wed them to predestination, a great number have made their escape into Asia, as also the Grand

Seignior. Some say it is to avoid the flail of pestilence; others say it to be through the fear they are in of the revolted troops : nay, some will need affirm, that the Ottoman Empire was reduced to the bare city of Constantinople ; that all the Pachas are revolted ; that the Grand Seignior himself was fled into Asia ; and that nothing reigned there but disorder and confusion. But as our accounts thence still vary, other advices tell us that the new Grand Vizier's* ministry had not been disturbed by any new revolt ; that by the prudence and vigour of his administration, he had reduced the greatest part of the mutineers to some state of submission and discipline; but at the same time confirm to us the Candian revolt, and massacre of their commanders, as also a deputation from the

* Mustapha Coprogli, the son of Achmet Coprogli, and grandson of Mahomet Coprogli, successively Grand Viziers, and two of the most admirable ministers in Turkish history. Mustapha was also a man of transcendant merit, perhaps even superior to his progenitors. He was killed at the battle of Salenkemen, which he had just gained against the Prince Lewis of Baden.

Divan of Egypt, with complaints against their Pacha's conduct, whom they accuse of espousing Mahomet the Fourth's* interests, and of using secret practices to fix a powerful party to restore him, or place one of his sons upon the throne; that as the projects for raising money had not the hoped-for success, so neither the army nor the fleet were in any reasonable posture; that, nevertheless, the Grand Seignior was hardly in any wise discomposed by all these distresses; that he was most taken up with the study of his law, leaving the management of affairs to his ministers; that he had been with several women, and that there was a report of three of them being with child, which is expected will dishearten Mahomet and his children's partizans, who are still under strict confinement; that the Ottoman Embassy to the Court of Persia had been fruitless, though

---

* Mahomet the Fourth was a weak and effeminate prince. He had been deposed on the 9th of November, 1687, when his brother, Soliman the Third, succeeded him. Soliman was indolent, superstitious, and almost imbecile. He died in 1691, just as measures were taking for deposing him.

the design of it was to engage the Sophy to fall upon the Muscovites, to make a diversion. The Persians are said indeed to have promised an irruption, but would not oblige themselves to it by any treaty.

We hear that the French before Algiers have shot 10,420 bombs into that place, that have reduced it to that condition, that the ruins of houses have stopped up all the streets; after which the French fleet is returned to Toulon, leaving only a number of ships to hinder the going in or out of those pirates.*

Great preparations are making on all hands for the meeting of the Parliament, and both Houses are said to be fitting up and beautifying for that purpose.

Colonel John Miller, eldest Captain of the Lord Craven's regiment, riding from the camp on Monday evening, is said by a fall from his horse to have lost his life.

---

* This expedition against Algiers had been conducted by the Marshal d'Estrées—who had bombarded the town in the manner described in this letter, on the 1st of July 1688.

A cherry-garden having tempted some soldiers into transgression, they were seized by the Provost and his men ; but some of their comrades offering at a rescue, were likewise taken up and punished.

Four fires have been within these three days; the last, in Catherine-street, on Tuesday, being the most considerable.   It burnt down the Fleece Tavern, with some adjoining houses, and is said to have been occasioned by the carelessness of a workman, leaving his glue-pot on the fire while he went to dinner, and which fired the shavings ; but what offers matter of discourse is, that a certain vintner, in disguise of a porter, coming to the assistance of the neighbourhood, conveyed away one hundred pounds to his own use, for which he is said to have been apprehended, and committed to the Gate-house.

A resort hath been this day or two to Totnam Court,* upon a silly rumour of an appa-

* Tottenham Court was a small estate and manor, close to London, which was at this time in the possession of the Du-

rition, and upon the finding in a pond parts of human bodies in barrels; but indeed it seems no more than a contrivance to get money.

Some difference is said to have arisen at Chatham between two Commanders of the navy, and that it hath occasioned their being both suspended, till his Majesty be fully informed of the matter.

Two ships being arrived from Bermudas, and supposed to have store of wreck-money on board, the King's broad arrow is said to be set upon them till such time as that they are brought to account. More ships are averred to be a money-fishing, but not without having first given the Duke of Albemarle security to render him a fair account and moiety of their prizes. The Prince of Wales having been somewhat indisposed at Richmond, occasioned a visit thither from their Majesties, and some

chess of Grafton, as heiress of Bennet Lord Arlington. From her it descended to the second Duke of Grafton, her son; and now belongs to the Lords Southampton, the first of whom was a younger son of that family.

stay. Orders are given for the embellishing the Princess of Denmark's Chapel in Whitehall; and as the work will be begun this week, it will be finished by the Court's return. Sir Richard Mason at Worster Park near Epsome, hath married his daughter to one Mr. Brownlow of the Temple; the lady having 1600*l.* portion, and the gentleman giving 300*l.* a-year pin-money, and 2000*l.* a-year jointure.

For John Ellis, Esq. Secretary to the
Commissioners for the Revenue of
Ireland,   At Dublin.

CLXI.

4th August, 1688

THE Prince hath been these ten days somewhat sick with the gripings, and put us into frequent alarms, but we hope all danger is passed. Last night happened an unlucky accident at Woolwich, where two men were a preparing some bombs, and happened to knock in the fuse with an iron hammer, which gave fire, and fired about 48 in all, besides some barrels of powder, dashed the workmen in pieces, and made a terrible fracas, and shattered, some say four, others more houses in the town. Our camp breaks up next week. The white staff or garter are not yet disposed of. I cannot tell you any thing certain of a Parliament; some think it may be off again. Pray give Mr. Smith your help in procuring me 4*l.* 5*s.* from a captain in that kingdom.

Mr. Ellis.

CLXII.

Judge Rotherham.—News foreign and domestic.—Prince of Wales recovered.

London, August 4th, 1688.

SIR,

WE have an account from several of the circuits, that the Judges are received in most places without any great pomp or numbers, and that at Berks and Oxford particularly, only the High Sheriff and his sons met them;

that both heard the sermon at St. Mary's, but that Judge Rothram* went afterwards to a private exercise of his own, where one Father Burgess, a well-gifted man, held forth before him, as he had done at Reading, where he told them the duty of Judges and Juries, especially at this conjuncture. The Judge accordingly gave his charge to the Jury, in which he much magnified the favour of the King's toleration, and inveighed as briskly against the Church of England and its clergy, who discover, he said, now the spirit of persecution, as much as others had done formerly, in matters of religion. He commended the law of the Lacedæmonians, which enjoins every man that imposes a new law, to try it first in his own family, and would have the Church of England do the same; then he fell upon the debaucheries of the clergy, how they run after vice, and in the midst of their laziness eat up the fat of the land; then he ripped up their stiffness and

* Serjeant Rotherham had just been made a Judge, for what reason is here evident.

disobedience, and instanced the late Bishops' petition, which he said was a libel, and he would be able to prove it so, if not more, for it tended to barr the prerogative, and alter the Government, which is treason; and it is said the Grand Jury, who were gentlemen of substance, and most of them Catholics, presented their Abhorrence of the said petition.

A warrant is granted out against the Earl of Denbigh's brother* and two other gentlemen, who are said to have rescued a fellow who had done some affront to Obadiah Walker of Oxford.

It is reported as if the deprived Fellows of Magdalen College intend to try their titles next term in Westminster Hall.

---

* William Fielding, only brother of Basil fourth Earl of Denbigh. He was at this time, it is presumed, an undergraduate at the University of Oxford. He married Lady Diana Newport, daughter to Francis Earl of Bradford, and widow of Thomas Howard, of Ashted in Surrey, Esq., and died September 21st, 1723. In 1716, he was constituted one of the Clerks Comptrollers of the Green Cloth.

We hear no more of a Parliament, though the Lords-Lieutenants are repaired into their counties, but no orders are yet given for the writs, though several fops write they will be issued out very speedily with a blank date.

The Earl of Maxfeild * hath not yet his pardon. Barnadiston is already come from Holland, and made his peace by an easy composition, by the means of a noble Catholic Lord.

Sir Josiah Child † is preparing a Relation of

* Gerard Earl óf Macclesfield.

† Sir Josiah Child, the eminent merchant, and ancestor of the Earls Tylney. He was now engaged in speculations in the East Indies. Evelyn gives the following account of his wealth and origin.

" March 16th, 1683, I went to see Sir Josiah Child's prodigious cost in planting walnut-trees about his seate (Wanstead), and making fish-ponds, many miles in circuit, in Epping Forest, in a barren spot, as oftentimes these suddainly monied men seate themselves. He, from a merchant's apprentice, and management of the East India Company's stock, being arrived (it is said) to an estate of 200,000l. He lately married his daughter to the eldest son of the Duke of Beaufort, late Marquis of Worcester, with 50,000l. portion at present, and various expectations." Burnet draws his character his late successes against the Great Mogoll, yet it is thought his rhetoric will scarce longer gain belief.   Since our Directions fall to the lowest ebb, and that we have but one ship come, and that not rich laden, whereas the Dutch have eleven in the country, without any shamming, Relations would be better argument to prove our good condition in those parts.

Captain Miller, in the Earl of Craven's regiment, mentioned in our last to fall from his horse coming from the camp; and it being dark, and his servant much in drink, he never recovered, but died the next day.

Some ships, as we also said in our last, are come from the West Indies, and the officers of

thus—" This summer (of 1699) Sir Josiah Child died.   He was a man of great notions as to merchandise, which was his education, and in which he succeeded beyond any man of his time.   He applied himself chiefly to the East India trade, which by his management was raised so high, that it drew much envy and jealousy both upon himself and upon the Company.   He had a compass of knowledge and apprehension, beyond any merchant I ever knew.   He was vain and covetous, and thought too cunning, though to me he seemed always sincere."

the Mint have been twice down the River to receive the King's share. The proprietors in Sir John Narborough's fishing will lose one-half of what it cost them this last year.

The Prince of Wales's indisposition on Tuesday last was occasioned by a great looseness, but is well recovered again.

The Duchess of Portsmouth is again returned into France, and great conjectures are made at her sudden departure.

The Bishop of Durham is expected suddenly in Court, to give his Majesty an account of what suspensions he hath made in the North for not reading the Declaration.

It is said the Duke of Modena* will have the blue garter, void by the death of the Duke of Ormond, which otherwise should have come to the Duke of Berwick.

* Francis II. of Este, Duke of Modena, brother of the Queen of James the Second. He did not succeed to the Duke of Ormonde's blue ribbon. At this time there were two *cordons* vacant, which were conferred, on the 28th of September, on the Dukes of Ormonde and Berwick.

The horse, and part of the foot, decamp from Hounslow next Wednesday.

The German army is said to have found a passage in the Save, which is good luck, and will put them in a condition of surprising the Turks at Belgrade.

They still discourse that the Great Turk is much uneasy under the vexations of his Government, though he dares not show it; and having left all to the disposal of his Grand Vizier, hath betaken himself to the study of the law and to his women, whereof three are already said to be big, to the great joy of his confidents.

The Cardinal of Furstemberg is said to be in disgrace in the Court of France, for having suffered the King to be slurred in the business of Cologne, by covetously pocketing most of the lewis-d'ors allowed for that purpose.

There fell lately vast numbers of caterpillars and other vermin in Languedoc, and other places of France.

We hear no perfect account of the earthquake at Rome, Madera, and Canaries, which, if true, will make indulgences and sweet wines very dear.

We hear just now from Woolwich, that some bombs that were there preparing, having accidentally taken fire, had done great mischief; more of which with the certainty in our next.

For John Ellis, Esq. Secretary to the
Commissioners for the Revenue of
Ireland,　　　　　At Dublin.

CLXIII.

Prince of Wales again ill.—Disaffection in the country.—Foreign news.

London, August 7th, 1688.

SIR,

THEIR Majesties have passed three or four days at Richmond with the Prince of Wales, his Royal Highness having continued indisposed by the gripes and looseness. Seral consults of doctors, and midwives, and nurses, have been had, and at last it was resolved his Highness should have the breast ; and a fresh countrywoman hard by was had on Saturday, and he hath since sucked, and been much better.

The Queen is resolved to continue with the Prince at Richmond, till he be well and in a condition to be removed to Windsor.

Councils and committees were put off at Windsor by reason that the King was with the Prince at Richmond.

The horse decamp next Wednesday, and are to go into their several quarters and garrisons in order to keep the peace and good order at the approaching elections for Parliament, though it be not yet certain that any directions are given for the Parliament writs.

Mr. Bernard Howard* is said to have brought two loyal addresses from Winchester, both signed by himself and others. The Grand Juries refused to pass an Abhorrence of the

* Bernard Howard was the eighth son of Henry Frederick, Earl of Arundel, and of his wife, Elizabeth Stuart, daughter of Esme Duke of Lennox. He was the direct ancestor of the present Duke of Norfolk.

Bishops' late petition, but were like to turn it into a presentment of another nature; that is, against such Roman Catholics as are in commissions of the peace, &c.

We have yet no certain account what the answers of the Archdeacons, Chancellors, and Commissaries, will be about reading the Declaration. As the day of their return draws nigh, so the town begins to be filled with clergymen, who come to expect the Lords' determination in the matter.

Great exceptions are taken by the several counties against the Judges, who arraign the Bishops in their charges at the circuit sessions, after they have been fairly acquitted by a trial and a verdict in the King's Bench.

Some of the Judges are said to have behaved themselves lukewarmly in the matter, and to have foreseen, at least forethought, of what disservice to the Crown a general discontent may prove to be; so that we may expect some farther change in Westminster Hall the next term.

The Duke of Lorraine* is so well recovered, that he takes the air in his calèche, and it is observed that he is very uneasy since the Elector of Bavaria is gone by to the army, being jealous lest the Elector should have the glory

* Though some account of Charles the Fifth, Duke of Lorraine, has been given in a preceding note, the following curious character of him by an illustrious contemporary may not be unacceptable to the reader: " Maintenant voici le portrait du Duc de Lorraine : la taille du Prince Radzivil, Maréchal de Lithuanie, les traits du visage de Chetmaki, et à peu près le même age que lui ; le nez très-aquilain, et presque en perroquet. Il est fortement marqué de la petite verole, et encore plus voûté que l'epine ; habit gris, sans ornement, si ce n'est des boutons de passementerie assez neufs ; chapeau sans plumes ; bottes jaunes, ou plutôt qui l'ont été il y a trois mois ; un cheval de combat passable, mais la bride et tout le harnais communs et usés, ainsi que la selle. Avec tout cela, il n'a pas la mine d'un marchand, mais d'un homme comme il faut, et même d'un homme de distinction. Il parle très bien de tout ce qui est de son ressort ; d'ailleurs, il est peu causeur, et paraît très-modeste. C'est, à propremet parler, un galant homme, qui entend la guerre parfaitement, et s'y applique sans relâche. Il porte une perruque blonde des plus malfaites ; en général, il est peu soucieux de sa mise, mais c'est un homme avec qui je m'accorderai tres-facilement, et qui est digne d'un sort plus haut." Lettres de Jean Sobieski à sa femme.

of happily concluding the campaign and the war together, by taking of Belgrade.

The Turks are said to offer fair conditions to the Emperor; but it being in the heat of a campaign, it looks like an amazement, besides that they would have a present cessation of arms to be one.

The Minister of Bavaria hath protested in the Diet of the Empire against the pretended election (or postulation) of the Cardinal of Furstembergh. We have not yet any account which way the Pope is, or when he is like to give his decision.

It is said, that some sudden orders called the French fleet from before Algiers, and that a part may be sent to Cadiz, or upon some other errand.

Our squadron is still in the Downs.

For John Ellis, Esq. Secretary to the
   Commissioners for the Revenue of
   Ireland,   At Dublin.

CLXIV.

Account of an Irish Watering-place.

Wexford, 7th August, 1688.

DEAR SIR,

HAD this place afforded me any thing worth communicating to you, I should have paid you my respects before now : this rendez-vous of decrepids, where people entertain one another with histories of their several ails and infirmities, enough if put together to make a second Wiseman's book of Martyrs, and talk nothing but the jargon of the place, of salts and minerals, volatile spirits, vomits, stools, tinging, precipitating, passing, or, as the ladies say, rendering :* then for dry roasted mutton, and rabbits, and chickens without sauce, and to be kept waking, as they try witches. And fantastical ladies, and fops, and lampoons in Wexford doggrel, would be an entertainment to you as bad as drinking the waters them-

* The town of Wexford, in the county of that name, possesses a mineral well, which is called " The Spa ;" at the time this letter was written it was much frequented, which is no longer the case.

selves. But with all this, I thank God I have made a considerable improvement in my health, and would gladly stay till Saturday sevennight, if I were not wanted. I beg you to give my duty to the Commissioners, and readiness to obey their commands, if required to come sooner; though I shall be tempted to return with the Bishop of Kilmore in the beginning of next week, for the convenience of his coach; but am not resolved. Lord Chancellor* goes hence to-morrow, the waters having agreed with him extraordinarily. I have desired Mr. Searl to wait upon you about an affair of my own, in which I dare assure myself of your kindness. Please to give Mr. Smith my hearty service, and accept of the same from,

Dear Sir,

Your most faithful,

Humble Servant,

JA. BONNELL.

Not a word of Mr. Hodson here, though a letter lies for him.

* Sir Alexander Fitton.

Pray let Mr. Farel know I had his letter.   I beg that Mr. Eckersal may give Mrs. Peppard my service; and an account of mine and Dr. King's health.

To John Ellis, Esq. Secretary to the
   Chief Commissioners of the Revenue, at the Custom-house,
                  Dublin.

CLXV.

A wet nurse procured for the Prince of Wales.—News
and accidents of various kinds.

London, August 9th, 1688.

SIR,

AT Richmond the Prince of Wales continues to suck the nurse allowed him, and it hath that good effect which is natural and usual to children; and their Majesties returned thence this day to Windsor. The nurse is the wife of a tile-maker, and seems a healthy woman; she came in her cloth petticoat and waistcoat, and old shoes and no stockings, but she is now rigged by degrees, (that the surprise may not alter her in her duty and care,) a 100*l.* per annum is already settled upon her, and two or three hundred guineas already given, which she saith that she knows not what to do with.

Yesterday morning about three or four o'clock died that pains-taking Henry Carre,* author of the late Pacquett of Advice from Rome, and of the Weekly Occurrences; some of our chief newsmongers are posted to Windsor to put in for his places.

The Judges at Oxford made strict enquiry after those scholars who had rescued the Townesends from the constable for abusing of Obadiah Walker; and the High Sheriff of the county recommended it to their lordships' cares in an elegant but short speech he made in court to this effect: "*Pray, my Lord, let's have Justice, or else good night Nicholas.*"

The Marchioness of Powys hath had a privy seal for 10,000*l.* to be paid her with-

* One of the newspaper-writers of the day.

out account, to be laid out for the use of the Prince of Wales.

We hear his Royal Highness is to be proclaimed and registered upon the Council-book of Ludlow, though he be not likely to be created yet some years, and the Duke of Beaufort is continued Lord President.*

The Lord Chancellor went on Monday morning towards Canterbury, to visit his brother who is one of the prebendaries there ; his lordship passes thence to Dover to wait on the Countess of Pembroke,† who embarks for France.

His Majesty dined yesterday at the camp, and saw the right wing, horse and foot, decamp, and march off towards the quarters allotted them.

It proves but too true what we have already mentioned, that at Woolwich some part of the

* Of Wales.

† Henrietta de Querouaille, sister of the Duchess of Portsmouth, and widow of the seventh Earl of Pembr o k. Her only daughter had just married the Chancellor's only son.

magazine is blown up by the carelessness of some of the workmen, who, contrary to their orders, used iron hammers instead of wooden ones about the granado shells, which they were a-making; but the poor men paid for their negligence with their lives; one of them being cut in the middle, and another having his head blown off; several others are wounded, and some houses blown up, one piece of the bombs shearing in two the cable of a ship that rode on the other side of the river.

A Mandamus is gone down for a Doctor's degree to Mr. Hall, Bishop elect of Oxford. His curate at Alhallowes-Stayning puts in hard to succeed him there, but it is thought he will keep it by commendam.

The Churchwardens of Oxfordshire were summoned to Oxford to give an account who read the Declaration; but being all come, nobody asked them the question, for it seems they were not sent for by the Chancellor.

About 11 o'clock last night, a fire broke out near Bennet's Castle, burning down about sixty houses, and several persons perishing in this sad occasion ; among whom, honest Clowsly of the Swan, is much lamented.

For John Ellis, Esq. Secretary to the
Commissioners for the Revenue of
Ireland, At Dublin.

CLXVI.

Court news.—Affairs of the East India Company.—Successes of the Imperialists against the Turks, &c.

London, Aug. 14th, 1688.

SIR,

ON Saturday last, his Royal Highness the Prince of Wales was removed from Richmond to Windsor, where he is lodged in the Princess of Denmark's house (which was Mrs. Ellen Gwyn's*), and is well recovered of his late indisposition, to the joy of the whole Court and kingdom.

* Nell Gwynn, the well-known mistress of Charles the Second.

His Highness's nurse is also in health and good plight, being kept to her old diet and exercise. She hath also a governess allowed her (an ancient gentlewoman), who is with her night and day, at home and abroad.

Last week arrived from the East Indies one Dr. St. Johns, who has been there for some years as Judge of the Admiralty for the East India Company. He is said to give an account of affairs in those parts, that is quite different from what was published in the Gazette, and not at all comfortable for the nation, at least for those concerned in the same bottom with the Company. The said Doctor attended the King in Council last Sunday in Windsor, where the matter of his information depends. He hath also some complaints of his own against the chief of that Company, who have of their own heads (and without any orders from his Majesty) taken away the Doctor's commission, which was under the Great Seal—but of this more hereafter. But it animates already a great grumbling in the City against a certain great

East India merchant, whose first name rhymes with Goliah.*

We hear every post some little advantages which the Imperialists have against the Turks. The Germans are passed the Save, and have taken a strong palank near Belgrade. They were but 8 or 900 men in all. There came 6000 Turks to make head against them, who of a sudden, fearing some trap or ambuscade was laid for them, were seized with such a fright, that they fled back to Belgrade, and left 1200 dead behind them, and the Germans masters of the place. The relation is so strange and seemingly improbable, that it will want a confirmation, though there be letters of it come from General Ashenhurst, who commanded the party.

The same letters say that Yeghen Pacha was at last come up to Belgrade, the peace and friendship between him and Osman, Pacha of that place, being thought to be made up. The

* Sir Josiah Child.

first thing he did was to proclaim himself Seraskier, and then endeavoured, but missed narrowly, to seize Osman in his tent. These new animosities being broke out, will likely disconcert all the forces the Turks have in those parts, and turn their swords against themselves, so that the Germans may promise themselves good success.

Till the issue of Belgrade be over, the Emperor will not give any answer to the conditions of peace said to be offered him.

The Janizaries of Candia have cut the throats of all their officers, and sent to the Doge Morosini * to offer him the Island, upon condition he will transport all the Turks into Asia, which no doubt will be easily granted.

The French letters give but little hopes that the Pope will be brought to confirm the

* Francis Morosini, who had previously gained much reputation by his successes against the Turks in the Morea, had just been elected Doge of Venice. At the time of his promotion he was employed in commanding the Venetian fleet in the Gulf of Egina. He died January 6th, 1694, at Napoli di Romania.

Cardinal of Furstemberg in the election of Cologne; and if the most Christian King be as zealous and resolute for the Cardinal, as the Emperor, they say, will be for Prince Clement, that matter may yet cause some bloody noses ere it be ended.

Just upon the coming away of our Flanders letters, an express is said to be arrived with an account that the election of Liege was over; that the Grand Dean was chosen Prince and Bishop; and thus the Cardinal baffled in all his new pretensions, but more of this hereafter.

The Prince of Orange is now forming a camp near Mastricht; and it is said the Elector of Brandeburgh and other neighbour princes are to have bodies of men within call, to join if there shall be occasion.

For John Ellis, Esq. Secretary to the Commissioners for the Revenue of Ireland,   At Dublin.

CLXVII.

Trial between Sheriff Firebrace and Mr. Brett.—
Various news.

London, August 16th, 1688.

SIR,

THIS day at ten of the clock, the Lords Commissioners for Ecclesiastical causes met at the Council-chamber in Whitehall, to receive the returns made by the several Chancellors and Archdeacons about reading the King's Declaration. The returns made are said to be satisfactory, but are kept private, of which we shall give a better account in our next.

The difference between Sheriff Firebrass and Mr. Brett, about the money lost by the first to the last at play, hath been heard in the Court of King's Bench and in Chancery, and in both courts the case seemed favourable for Sir Basill;* though he it was that lost the money to the value of 2900 guineas, and then is said by

* Sir Basil Firebrace.

force to have taken away above one-half from
Brett, the winner. The Lord Chancellor, the
last term, referred the matter to themselves to
be amicably made up ; but since, it is said,
some of the chief witnesses for Sir Basill, particularly his butler, had tacked about, and do
retract what they once swore for Firebrass, and
do begin to swear for Brett ; and so the matter may have farther consequences · than was
at first thought of.

Mr. Weston, an iron-merchant, did narrowly
escape destruction at the unhappy accident at
Woolwich, where he happened to be when the
magazine blew up, and was in a room whence
he could not have escaped, if a bomb had not
blown down the side of a house and made way
for him. In consideration of this deliverance,
he is about settling a sermon to be preached
upon that day for ever, at his parish church in
London, and another at Woolwich, and intends
some farther charity to the poor.

Clowsley, at the Swan in Fish-street, was
buried three nights ago with great decency and

good order, the members of most of the public offices about the town being invited, and a notable sermon was preached upon the text of the falling of the Tower of Siloam. The damages of that fire are reckoned to be 30,000*l*.

The Right honourable the Lord Dartmouth, who is indefatigable in the King's service, went yesterday down the River, to view some places made upon the river, where the platforms are to be built for the security of the Navy Royal at Chatham.

The Marquess d'Albeville, his Majesty's Envoy in Holland, is arrived, and gone to wait on the King at Windsor.

The French letters confirm what we writ in our last, that the lot in the election at Liege was fallen upon the Baron de Elderen, the Grand Dean, who is a native of Brabant; and so the Cardinal of Furstemberg is foiled out of all share in the spoils of the late Elector of Cologne.

The French King hath given orders for the raising of 10,000 foot and 6000 horse, and hath sent his commands to all his officers to be ready and upon their guard.

All letters agree that Candia* is reduced under the Venetians; so the Doge Morosini hath recovered in a day, without blood or expense, a place that cost so much of both when it was lost, and is of the greatest importance to the trade of Christendom.

For John Ellis, Esq. Secretary to the
    Commissioners for the Revenue of
    Ireland,   At Dublin.

CLXVIII.

Foreign news.—King gone to see his ships.—Ecclesiastical
Commission.

London, August 18th, 1688.

SIR,

THE Gazette gives an account how that the rich widow Princess of Radzivil baulked

---

* If the Venetians had succeeded at this moment in recovering part of the Island of Candia, it did not remain long in their possession, since the Turks, in the course of this war,

the Prince of Poland,* and is married to the Prince Palatine: it may be added, how the French Ambassador in the Court of Berlin was so far surprised with this sudden match, that he thrust himself into the room where the married couple were, with a design to break off the marriage, but found them just a-dressing after they had been a-bed and consummated the marriage. How Prince Jacob† of Poland will resent the loss of his mistress, time must tell us.

The French begin to fail of their usual success elsewhere also; for, as they failed in this love-intrigue, we have it from all hands confirmed they did the like in the elections of Cologne, Munster, and Liege, where the Dean was chosen; so, as we have already said, the

conquered the whole of it, with the exception of the fortresses of Suda and Spinalonga, and it has remained ever since under their domination.

* For an account of this transaction, see note †, at page 87.

† Meaning James.

Cardinal of Furstemberg had no share in the feathers of the dead Elector.

The Pope is said to have sent his Bull in favour of Prince Clement's election ; and the French King has ordered 10,000 foot and 6000 horse to be raised, which the world believes are designed in favour of the Cardinal. The Dutch on their post stand upon their guard, and are to have 20,000 men encamped near the frontiers, to watch the motions of their neighbours.

The Pope hath excommunicated Mons[r]. Talon, the French Advocate-general, who made the late speech in favour of the King, against his Holiness, in the matter of the Franchises.

His Majesty goes next Tuesday down the River to Portsmouth, where the squadron of ships now at sea will meet his Majesty, and orders are given for fitting some more ships to be ready upon occasion. The Dutch are also said to be refitting several of their biggest ships.

The Queen Dowager intends to live sometimes out of London, and has sent to view

Knole,* the Earl of Dorset's† house in Kent, which has more rooms than any house in England.

The University of Oxford has appointed a deputation of doctors and others, who are to be in London next week, to install the Duke of Ormond their Chancellor.

The Lords for Ecclesiastical Causes met the 16th, and received the few returns that were made about reading the Declaration. Many of the Chancellors attended in person, and sent word they had no returns, but were there ready if the Lords had any thing to say to them.

Dr. Wainwright, of Chester, and Dr. Paine,

* Knowle near Sevenoaks, the ancient seat of the Sackvilles.

† Charles (Sackville) sixth Earl of Dorset, the celebrated wit of the time of Charles the Second. Lord Orford says of him that, "He was the finest gentleman in the voluptuous court of Charles II. and in the gloomy one of William. He had as much wit as his first master, or his contemporaries Buckingham and Rochester, without the royal want of feeling, the Duke's want of principles, or the Earl's want of thought." He died January 25th, 1706, leaving behind him an only son, subsequently created Duke of Dorset.

for Rochester, returned a few names that read; others sent up word, that they either never saw the Declaration, or saw it by chance, or saw not the order for reading it. This is but an uncertain account; the matter is kept private, and the Court adjourned to the 6th of December next.*

For John Ellis, Esq. Secretary to the
   Commissioners for the Revenue of
   Ireland,   At Dublin.

CLXIX.

Dutch fitting out ships.—News of various kinds, &c.

London, Aug. 21st, 1688.

SIR,

ALL the news at court and city at present is, that the Dutch are a-fitting out several capital ships; some say twenty, others thirty or forty in number; and that they are working at it night and day, as if they had some mighty en-

* The Ecclesiastical Commission never met again after this time.

terprise in hand, at least in their heads; though, all things considered, they cannot well put any ships at all to sea at this time, since the *banks* of their country are usually shut up with the frost in September: so that this equipage must be designed for the next year, though it may serve now to add weight and value to the States, who are entered into leagues with the Protestant Princes of Germany for the keeping of the peace, which is in some danger from the eager contests that are like to be about the election at Cologne.

Nor is there any good ground for another report that flies about, which is, that the Dutch are to send hither two ambassadors very speedily with some hasty message, being to stay when they are come but four or five days: this is some coffee-house discourse blown about to amuse the world.

To-morrow the Queen is to do the Lord Chancellor the honour to dine at Bulstrode, whither her Majesty goes attended with several of the chief ladies at Court.

K 2

His Majesty's progress to Portsmouth is put off for some longer time.

Last Thursday an officer of Colonel Kirk's* regiment wounded a waterman upon the Thames, for dashing of him with water; he is not yet dead, but the officer is said to abscond.

The Bishop of Chester's son had a Mandamus lately to All Souls in Oxon for a living which is in that college's gift, and is said to be resigned into the King's hand by the Bishop himself who enjoyed it: all the answer that the college is said to give is, that they will consider of it.

Next Thursday the Duke of Ormond keeps his Installation-dinner; several members of

---

* Kirk was an officer of ability, but had rendered himself infamous by the cruelties he had perpetrated in the West during Monmouth's rebellion; which Burnet attributes to his "having commanded so long at Tangier, that he was become savage by the neighbourhood of the Moors there." When James asked him to change his religion, he answered, that he was already pre-engaged, having promised the Emperor of Morocco, if ever he did change, to turn Mahometan.

the University of Oxon being to be then in town to perform that ceremony, amongst whom are to be Dr. Jane,* Dr. Wallis, Dr. Aldridge, Dr. Holton and others.

The Hague letters tell us of a Frenchman, that, under the disguise of a refuged Protestant, was a Papist, and betrayed all those that fled thither, wheedling them to tell him how they had escaped, and where their estates lay, and then giving notice of it to the French Ambassador. The States had knowledge of it, and sent to seize him ; but knowing his guilt, and being a desperate fellow, he chose to die rather than be taken.

We hear the Cardinal of Furstemberg hath new coaches making at Paris with the arms of the Elector upon them, which looks as if he were resolved to stand his ground whether the Pope says amen to it or no.

* Dr. Jane was one of the Whitehall preachers, and was the man who, with Patrick, argued before Lord Rochester against two Catholic Doctors upon the points of difference between the two religions.

The German army passed the Save the 28th of July, old style,* so that by this time the strength and fate of Belgrade is known in some measure; Count Tekely and a party of Tartars undertook to dispute the passage to them, but were glad to retreat in great confusion, and to get into Belgrade.

The Pacha of Egypt is said to have rebelled, and to have refused to send any men into the service of the Grand Seignior.

There has been a dismal earthquake at Smirna, which destroyed a great part of the city, and buried some of our English merchants under its ruins; and what makes it the more lamentable is, that a fire succeeding, was likely to consume all that remained; for the ship that brought those sad news left it still burning.

For John Ellis, Esq. Secretary to the
    Commissioners for the Revenue of
    Ireland,   At Dublin.

---

* On the 6th of August, Prince Lewis of Baden had completely defeated fifteen thousand Turks.

CLXX.

Prince and Princess at Tunbridge.—Ecclesiastical Commission adjourned.

Tunbridge, August 21st, 1688.

DEAR SIR,

THAT I do not weekly persecute you according to my old wont, you are in part beholden to my maladies, that have kept me here fourteen days, and in part to other avocations. For news, I cannot tell what to say at this distance from Court, though we have a faint representation of one here: her Royal Highness and Prince George,* whose stay has been a month, and is to extend a month longer. The world is surely running into a high bustle, and one year will let us see whose party is strongest; for my share, I know not what to wish or fear, I think even to drive adrift. Our Ecclesiastical Commission flags mightily

* The Princess Anne and her husband Prince George of Denmark. They were anxious at this time to be as much away from Court as possible.

in their work, as it should seem by the length of their adjournment to the 1st Thursday in December. The inclosed, I hope, will bring some money into your hands. I am wishing for 50*l.* there; do the utmost you can, pray, with Colonel Sarsefield.* Seal and send the inclosed. I shall be at London to-morrow, and not stir thence again ; so yours with the usual direction to be left with Mr. James Dalton at the General Post-office, will always find me. I would be glad to be your remembrancer to the Bishop, if I knew what to say; for Fr. Cave here, as well as my own imagination, tells me you are weary.

Yours always,

J. F.

Pray, if Dick Pine be killed, let me know what his widow, my countrywoman, is the better for it.

For John Ellis, Esq. Secretary of
 His Majesty's Revenue in Ireland,
 Ireland.   Dublin.

---

* Afterwards created Lord Lucan.

CLXXI.

Judge Allibone dead.—Earthquake at Smyrna.—Council at Windsor.—Foreign news.

London, Aug. 23d, 1688.

SIR,

WHEN the Lords Commissioners for Ecclesiastical Causes met last Thursday, there was no Judge present but Chief Justice Herbert, and no Bishop but he of Chester. The Bishop of Rochester* sent his excuse in a letter, that he could not come, and that it was not in his intention to act any more in the Commission, especially against those of his own order, the Bishops. (The letter was well penned.)

This looking like a disgust in that Bishop, there is the less opposition in the Bishop of Chester's way to the Archbishoprick of York.

Last night died Judge Allybone, at his house near Gray's-Inn. He was but newly returned home from his circuit; his death is said to be caused by a great cold which he took in passing through the wilds of Kent, as well as by

* Sprat.

his overheating himself by his vehemence in declaiming against the Bishops in his charge to the Juries.

The bad news from Smyrna continues yet, but our merchants hope it is not so bad as the first report made it; which said, that a terrible earthquake has overturned the foundations of all the town, and that a violent fire broke out, which with its sulphurous smell stifled those that had escaped from the ruins; that the first noise, which began with dismal groanings, came from a mountain which stands above the town, which is said to be all sunk excepting a little chapel which stands at one end of it, where St. John is said to have been frequent at the first beginnings of Christianity. But all will deserve a confirmation.

On Friday, that is to-morrow, is summoned a general Council to be held at Windsor, where it is believed his Majesty will be pleased to declare himself as to the day that the Parliament is to meet at Westminster.

The Windsor air begins to be sharp, and for

hat reason it is thought the Prince will not continue much longer there, but will be removed either to Richmond or rather to St. James's.

His Majesty has sent orders to all officers and soldiers to repair to their respective quarters; and some say the reason of it to be that he soldiers are rude in several places, and that his Majesty is troubled with frequent complaints against them.

Their Majesties did the Lord Chancellor the honour to dine at his house at Bulstrode, where there was a most splendid entertainment, befitting the royal guests, and his lordship's generosity and affection to the Crown.

We have nothing from Holland but new libels against his Majesty and his Government, and daily alarums of more ships a-fitting out; but though we have had indeed some instances to the contrary, yet September has been looked upon too late for a fleet to dance at sea, whatever the present intention may be; which a short time may disclose to us.

The next German letters may tell us something of Belgrade.   The army passed the Save the 29th past, old style, and found little resistance.   The Elector of Bavaria showed great, some think desperate, resolution, in marching 500 only of his troops over the river, where were at least 8 or 10,000 to resist them : the Duke of Lorraine's friends were against it ; and the Duke himself is so fond of glory that he is resolved for the army, and ot share that of taking Belgrade with the Elector.   The Queen Duchess is as fond of the Duke, and resolved to follow him to the army, considering his ill state of health ; but the Emperor has laid his commands upon her not to go beyond Buda.   A Turkish Chiave was in his way to Buda with conditions of peace, and the Emperor's Commissioners were a-going to meet and treat with them.

For John Ellis, Esq. Secretary to the
  Commissioners for the Revenue of
  Ireland,   At Dublin.

CLXXII.

Duke of Ormonde receives the University Deputation.—Dutch Preparations.—Parliament to be summoned.—Belgrade taken.

London, August 25th, 1688.

YOURS of the 14th came to me at my L^d. D. of Ormonde's when I was going amongst above 500 more, to sit down to dinner on Thursday. They were highly treated, and took it as well. The Vice-Chancellor Ironside made him a short speech, and the Elder Proctor a longer; eloquent enough, and the compliments well couched. His Grace answered short in English. He hath writ his acceptance of the favour they have done him on your side; but it had been purer if they had not doubted, for Nature never formed a more undaunted and settled resolution to support the cause he pretends to serve. I suppose upon the receipt of his he is declared, and all matters settled relating thereto. We are wonderfully in the dark here what is like to happen. The Dutch are putting out nine capital ships : they have great

quantities (8000) of arms aboard, and accoutrements for 4000 horse.   The French King hath
sent an advertisement that it is designed an
invasion upon us, and the Manifesto thereupon
is already here, and passeth privately amongst
his well-willers.   The King says he cannot imagine the aim, and yet I find some of our noblemen suspected of strange, unnatural dealing.*
Some ten of our great ships are fitting with
all haste, and our fleet come to the Buoy of
the Nore.   They work day and night at the
rest of their great ships in Holland, and put
them over the pampus as they are ready.   Prince
of Orange hath taken up 300,000*l.* upon his own
credit.   These preparations are managed by a
secret Committee of seven, all confidents of

* Lords Mordaunt, Shrewsbury, Delamere, Derby, Nottingham, Lumley, Devonshire, Harry Sydney, Admiral Russell, the Bishops of London and Bristol, three of the principal
General officers of the Army, Trelawney, Kirk, and Lord
Churchill, and many others of different degrees were at this
time in correspondence with the Prince of Orange, and urging
him to come over to England, though certainly not as yet
with any view of making him King.

the Prince's and the States have reposed such a
trust, that they are accountable to none for
their actions.   The French army are marched,
and that King hath made eighty General-
officers, whereof nineteen Lieutenant-generals ;
and the Germans are marching too to join the
Dutch army : never more appearance of a
severe war; you may believe our Court very
anxious.   Yesterday was for a General Council
about the Parliament, according to conjecture.
The young Prince is very lively and sucks
strongly, but seems withal to be asthmatic.
An Eschevin at St. Omer's is sent bound hand
and foot to Paris, a design being discovered
of betraying Calais to the Dutch, as the King
thinks : most of this foreign account is from
his own mouth yesterday, after reading his
letters.   Russell, I believe, will have the regiment of horse, (and then desired to sell it
though) ; the engines be against him.   I will
do my best for you with Rene Grahme, but I
have a debt of my own there, which I have
not asked him for these seven years.   I have

put the like trouble upon you to Sarsefield and Aunt Eustace.

Yesterday, a Council was held at Windsor about the calling a Parliament; the Lord Chancellor was very warm with Lord President against it, but was over-ruled: so the writs are to issue the 18th of Oct. and the Parliament to meet 27th Nov. This evening an express from Flanders went to the King, with the news of Belgrade's* being taken without any loss on the Christians' part.

For John Ellis, Esq. Secretary of
His Majesty's Revenue in Ireland,
Ireland.   At Dublin.

CLXXIII.

St. James's, August 26th, 1688.

DEAR BROTHER,

COLONEL DEMPSY would not go without a letter from me to you. I received a long

* Belgrade was not taken till the 6th of September, when the Elector of Bavaria, at the head of the Imperial troops, gained possession of it by assault. This account probably alluded to some of the forts or outworks belonging to it.

one lately from you, which my weakness will not permit me to answer yet : it is only an accidental indisposition, caused by a long journey ; when I am able, I will give you a farther account of things, and of myself, being,

Dear Brother,

Your affectionate Brother, and

Humble Servant,

ELLIS.*

Remember me to brother William.   We all here are well, and the Prince very particularly ; but something alarmed at the Holland preparations.

To John Ellis, Esq. Secretary to his
   Majesty's Commissioners for the
   Revenue in Ireland,
           At Dublin.

---

* The signature of Philip Ellis, the Popish Bishop.

CLXXIV.

Increase of Irish Revenue.—Praise of the Duke of Ormonde.

Cornbury, August 27th, 1688.

SIR,

YOUR's of the 6th instant came to me hither, where I have been upon my private affairs about a fortnight, and shall not be at London till about a fortnight hence; so that you will not expect I should entertain you much from hence. I am very glad the Revenue there holds up so wonderfully: it is indeed very extraordinary the Customs Inwards should swell, when trade visibly decays, and the consumption lessens, which seem to be contradictions; God send the Revenue may not sink on a sudden! Your University * could not have done better than in choosing the Duke of Ormond their Chancellor, as ours has done, which pleaseth all good men. Too much honour and respect cannot be conferred on that family; and none has more reason to reverence it than those in Ireland, whose ingratitude makes them pleased at his death; but the late Duke's me-

* The University of Dublin.

mory will live for ever among all honest Englishmen ; and this present Duke will worthily support the glory of his great name.   When I am in town I shall write more largely to you, as occasion offers ; at present I shall only assure you that I am very truly,

Sir,

Your most affectionate Servant,

CLARENDON.

Pray do me the kindness to let the inclosed be delivered to my good Lord Longford, with my most humble service.

For John Ellis, Esq. Secretary to the
Commissioners of the Revenue in
Ireland,   Dublin.

CLXXV.

The French King expostulates with the Dutch on their preparations.—Other Foreign news.—Lord Mayor thrown from his horse.

London, Aug. 30th, 1688.

SIR,

THE Lord Dartmouth is gone down to Chatham, to give the necessary orders for equip-

L 2

ping of ten men of war more, which will be ready in three weeks' time.

The French King is said to have ordered his Ambassador in Holland to expostulate with the Dutch about the design of their present arming by sea and land; with this intimation, that he will look upon the first step they make against any of his allies to be against himself, and a breach of the peace; and will thereupon march 50,000 men into their country. The Dutch, on their side, have also sent to their Ambassador at Paris, to desire the French King to take off the new impositions he has lately laid upon their commodities, as herrings, cloth, &c. and to release some Dutch ships that have been long arrested in France; otherwise, that they will be forced to grant reprisals to their subjects. We must expect the answer of either side.

In the mean time the Prince of Orange is at his camp with 20,000 men, and a good body of artillery; and letters from the Empire tell us that several of those next adjacent Princes are marching such bodies of their troops towards the Rhine, as will, with the Dutch forces, make up 60,000 men, which the Prince of Orange is to command in chief.

Some letters tell us, that the Pope has absolutely confirmed the election of Prince Clement, and given no other answer to the French party who solicited for the Cardinal, than that he wondered how the King of France comes to meddle in elections within the Empire, and how Furstemberg, being already Cardinal and Bishop of Strasburgh, comes to desire more benefices.

The Dolphin * is to have an army under his command; and most people think he will march towards Switzerland, and may have a design upon Geneva.

Some thousands of Suisses are put into

* "The Dolphin" means the Dauphin, commonly called the Grand Dauphin, only son of Lewis the Fourteenth; who died during the lifetime of his father.

Dunkirk and Calais; and several officers in these places are said to be sent up to Paris in custody.

Sir John Shorter,* the present Lord Mayor, lies very ill with a fall off his horse, under Newgate, as he was going to proclaim Bartholomew fair. The City custom is, it seems, to drink always under Newgate when the Lord Mayor passes that way; and at this time the Lord Mayor's horse being somewhat skittish, started at the sight of a large glittering tankard which was reached to his Lordship.

The next Lord Mayor, it is said, will be Sir John Isles, an anabaptist; and Alderman Thompson and Edwynne, to be Sheriffs.

The African Company is said to have put a

* Sir John Shorter was the son of John Shorter, Esq. of Staines, in Middlesex, and of a grandaughter of Lord Forbes, of the kingdom of Scotland. Sir John was ancestor, by his two grandaughters, of the Walpoles, Earls of Orford, of the first creation; and of the Seymours, Marquises of Hertford. Sir John Shorter died of the fall here mentioned, as will be seen by a subsequent letter.

stop to the payment of any money for the present out of their stock.

For John Ellis, Esq. Secretary to the
   Commissioners for the Revenue of
   Ireland,   Dublin.

CLXXVI.

Duke of Ormonde.—Mr. Chudleigh, &c.

30th August, 1688.

DEAR SIR,

I RECEIVED last night together both your letters of the 15th and 23rd: where the first lay so long, I am not able to tell you; I am sure I am glad it came at last. Mr. Lowndes, who keeps all the Irish Papers, is out of town; when we come together again, I will get you a copy of Mr. Galway's thirty-nine articles, which are very long; but I am in hopes that I may see you suddenly here, and then I will put those papers into your hands. What I hear of the increase of your Revenue is very extraordinary, but I fancy it were not difficult to find the reason of it, especially if it happens upon the Customs. James Clarke and his wife send you their affectionate services: they have taken the next house to your friend Mr. Chudleigh, where they will always be glad to see you. The good Duke of Ormonde hath no farther service for him ; his Grace continues all his grandfather's officers in the principality of Tipperary, and commissions for them went away yesterday. If I had a good conveyance, I could send as good a story as yours of the 23rd of August, and much to the same purpose ; but that shall serve us to talk of. Mr. Chud. is going out of England in three or four days, in discontent I fear : he hath parted with every servant he kept here. I was last night standing at James Clarke's door, and I see him come out of his in very great ceremony, with a couple of priests. I was to wait on him. He told me he thought he should pass this winter at Paris, though I hear it will be at Rome. I received last night the inclosed for you from

Cornbury.   My wife and her sister send you their humble services; and I am with all my heart,

Dear Sir,

Your most faithful humble servant,

WM. SHAW.

Mr. J. Ellis.

For John Ellis, Esq. Secretary to the
Commissioners of his Majesty's Revenues of Ireland,   Dublin.

CLXXVII.

Naval preparations on all sides.—News from France and
Turkey.—Medal respecting the Seven Bishops.

London, Sept. 1st, 1688.

SIR,

ALL hands are at work here, as well as with our neighbours, in fitting out ships to sea. His Majesty's fleet will be increased to about thirty-two ships, and it is said the Lord Dartmouth is to command the same as Admiral, by whose care and diligence, next that of his

Majesty, these ships are rigged out with so much expedition. It is also talked, as if his Majesty intended to give his Lordship an additional honour of an Earl,* as a farther mark of his favour.

The Dutch fleet rides still before the Maze, and fresh ships are added to it with speed from the several places that are obliged to furnish the same: the town of Amsterdam hath equipped twelve for their proportion.

Seamen are wanting everywhere; and as they flock but tardily to the English fleet, so the Dutch are forced to use all arts to debauch our mariners, by rewards, promises, and a good salary. The French Protestants are very ready and forward for any expedition.

We may expect ere long some declaration or other from the French Ambassador at the Hague, upon the subject of their land and sea

---

* The Lord Dartmouth in question, who was the first Lord of that title, was never created an Earl. His son, however, received that honour from the hands of Queen Anne, Sept. 5, 1711.

reparations ; and foreign news-letters give out that the Princes of the Rhine have a number of troops already in march to join the Dutch, and that others are invited into the alliance, particularly the Kings of Denmark and Sweden ; and that a body of Swedes are to be put on board the Dutch fleet, whenever they sail.

Notwithstanding the fair prospect we had of an accommodation between the Court of Rome and France, our late French letters almost cramp the hopes of it. They tell us that the Marquis of Croissy* went to the Cardinal-Nuncio in the Christian King's name, and told him that, his Majesty having been informed that the Pope had ordered a reward for such as should bring in two of the Marquis de Lavarlin's† officers alive or dead, he let him know that in case any misfortune befell them, the

* Charles Colbert de Croissi, brother of the great Colbert. He had been employed with credit in several embassies, and was now Secretary of State for Foreign Affairs, in which situation he had succeeded Arnaud de Pomponne, in 1679. He died in 1696.

† The French Ambassador at Rome.

King would cause two to be chosen out of the Nuncio's, who should be served in the like manner ; and that in case the Ambassador was attacked, they should be indispensably obliged to attack the person of the Nuncio, to give him the same treatment.

His Eminency made answer, that he was Nuncio, and was acknowledged as such by his Majesty ; whereas the Marquis of Lavardin was but a private person, neither having been owned nor received by the Pope ; and that the difference was great between them two.

The Marquis of Croissy replied, that the quality of Ambassador was given by those that send them, and not by those that received them.

The Nuncio told him, he was ready to be gone, and return into Italy ; but De Croissy retorted, that he must have a care of stirring from Paris, or any of his domestics ; and that he let him know this in the King his master's name ; and that otherwise other measures should be taken.

We have no farther account of the Turkish peace, the Emperor being not willing to give his answer upon the condition offered, till he has consulted with his allies.

The fair weather may invite the Court to stay some longer time than was once intended at Windsor.

The Duke of Albemarle and his consociety have a new patent passing for them for fishing upon any wreck in the West Indies, within a year, beginning the 20th of Aug. 1688.

His Majesty has granted a charter of Incorporation to the French Protestants lately come over, with power to build a church for themselves.

A medal is said to run about with the Seven Bishops on one side, with these words ; *"Wisdom hath built her house, and chosen out seven pillars ;"* on the other side, a church undermined by a Jesuit and a fanatic, with these words ; " *The gates of Hell shall not prevail against her.*"

The Lord Mayor lay dangerously ill with

his late bruise (or rather fright) by his fall, but is said now to be much better.

The report which we inserted in our last of the African Company having stopped the payment of any money, is false.

For John Ellis, Esq. Secretary to the
Commissioners for the Revenue of
Ireland,   At Dublin.

CLXXVIII.

Dutch Fleet and Army ready.

London, September 1st, 1688.

SOMETHING like your account of the 23d is not unknown to us here, though I think there is little credit now given by the people of most understanding to the apprehensions that the Dutch would invade here. They are not out yet, nor the spare arms and saddles aboard, but all of them, and what part of their army they please, may be so in forty-eight hours. I hear the Pope's decision is not come, and the

French King's orders not to do any violence till then. We think the Dutch will not be aggressors, which is in a good measure the ground of our security. Their confederates, and 25,000 of their own, will form them an army of 52,000 within ten days, on the Rhine; and I think 8000 of them may be spared to embark, and do much mischief about Rochell, &c. : this notion, and their coming out that they may not be caught tardy in the spring, is the last conjecture. The Dutch have twenty-two great ships in the Maas mouth, and brag of ninety-six to be in a fleet in six weeks. D. of Ormonde is at Badminton. We shall have thirty-eight ships and twelve fire-ships shortly abroad.

Yours,

J. F.

Rene Grahme and all other officers are at their places. Herbert * is at last declared Vice-

---

* " In July 1688, Admiral Herbert came over to Holland, and was received with a particular regard to his pride and ill-humour ; for he was upon every occasion so sullen and pee-vish, that it was plain he set a high value on himself, and

Admiral of North Holland, with 600*l.* per annum pension.

> For John Ellis, Esq. Secretary of His
>   Majesty's Revenue in Ireland,
> Ireland.   At Dublin.

expected the same of all others.   He had got his accounts passed, in which he complained that the King had used him not only hardly but unjustly.   He was a man delivered up to pride and luxury.   Yet he had a good understanding; and he had gained so great a reputation by his steady behaviour in England, that the Prince understood that it was expected he should use him as he himself should desire; in which it was not very easy to him to constrain himself so far as that required.   The managing him was in a great measure put on me; and it was no easy thing.   It made me often reflect on the providence of God, that makes some men instruments in great things, to which they themselves have no sort of affection or disposition; for his private quarrel with the Lord Dartmouth, who he thought had more of the King's confidence than himself had, was believed the root of all the sullenness he fell under towards the King, and of all the firmness that grew out of that."—Burnet.

CLXXIX.

Death of John Bunyan.—Roman Catholic Clergy confirm their youth.—Charter of Chester changed.—Various reports from abroad.

London, Sept. 6th, 1688.

SIR,

ON Tuesday last died, as we have said already, the Lord Mayor, Sir John Shorter: the occasion of his distemper was his fall under Newgate, which bruised him a little, and put him into a fever. His Lordship had a piece of helpless comfort brought him before he died, which was, that a Corn-meter's place, and that of the Common Hunt were fallen void the same day, which were worth to him, or rather his executors, 3000*l*. Few days before died Bunian,* his Lordship's teacher, or chaplain, a

---

* This was the celebrated John Bunyan, the apostle of the Baptists, and author, among many other works, of " The Pilgrim's Progress," the most popular book in the English language. He was a man of the most blameless life and character, and suffered much and long, on account of his religious opinions. He was the son of a tinker at Elstow, near Bedford. He died of a fever, at the age of sixty.

VOL. II.   M

man said to be gifted that way, though once a cobbler.

Another gentleman, lately one of the Commissioners for the Customs, hath quitted this world, though he hath not changed it for another. He hath stript himself of what necessaries were most cumbersome, and is a-going to France to be a Carthusian monk. He is said to have given his clerk money to pay his debts, and to qualify him to enter the same state, and to have left his goods, except his money and coach, to his friends.

A venomous report, without any truth in it, is spread about, as if some French troops were to land speedily, of which there is not the least appearance, there being not the least motion of those of his Majesty's own. And our French letters tell us, upon strict enquiry in all the sea-ports, that only some few thousands are come to the water-side, to reinforce their own garrisons, of which there is occasion, since the Dutch fleet is so strong, and to be one-third manned with French Hugonots that are re-fuged.

The Roman clergy about London, in imita-tion of the Protestant bishops, begin their several circuits very speedily, in order to con-firm their youth, and others of their com-munion.

The Charter of Chester is now passing the Seals; most of the old members are changed; Sir Thomas Stanley is Mayor, and Lord Bran-don Gerrard,* Recorder.

The French youths at Paris talk of nothing less than besieging Namur and Philipsburgh, and say the King will begin the dance in person : they will have four armies, one in Flanders, under Humières;† the second in Cologne, under Bouflers; the third in Germany, under Ma-réshal Duras; ‡ and the fourth towards Italy

* Lord Brandon was the eldest son of the Earl of Mac-clesfield.

† Lewis de Crevan, Marshal d'Humières, made a Mar-shal of France in 1668, died in 1694.

‡ James Henry de Durfort, Marshal de Duras, nephew of

and Suisse, under the Dolphin and the Duke of Savoy.*

The fine rich widow Princess Radzivil, who lately baulked the Prince of Poland, and was so smit with the Prince of Newburg as to marry him upon two days' acquaintance, is said to be already cold and disgusted in her affection, saying her husband is no man, and that her marriage is not yet consummated, and now cries out for the Prince of Poland again. If this be true, women may be deceived in men, as well as men in women : however, this great lady has furnished a curious subject for a pleasant amorous novel.

the great Turenne, and brother of the Marshal de Lorge and Lord Feversham ; made a Marshal in 1675, and died in 1704.

* Victor Amadeus the Second, Duke of Savoy, King of Sicily in 1713, which kingdom he was compelled to exchange for that of Sardinia in 1720, abdicated the throne in favour of his son in 1730, of which he immediately afterwards repented ; and died in 1732. He was a brave and able prince, but restless and faithless to the last degree ; which latter qualities occasioned his life to be one of constant trouble and unceasing vicissitudes.

Lord Spencer,* son to the Earl of Sunderland, lies a-dying, after a lingering distemper, at Paris.

The Venetians† expect daily the news that the Doge has taken some part of the Island Negropont, which was the old famous Euboea.

The Elector Palatin is said also to be dead,‡ who was father-in-law to the Emperor and King of Portugal; if so, the Duke of Lorraine has lost a great obstruction in his favour at the Imperial Court, this Elector having all along been his rival.

We do not hear the Dutch are come yet to any resolution about the forbidding of commerce with, or granting reprisals against, France. Brandy wine is so essential to the

* He died on the 5th of September.

† The Doge Francis Morosini had undertaken, in concert with Count Konigsmark, the siege of Negropont, the capital town of the Island of that name. The Count died during the siege, which Morosini was obliged to raise in the autumn, without having effected any thing.

‡ This was a false report, as Philip William, Elector Pala-ine, did not die till the year 1690.

Dutch Government, that this is not very probable; Germany and Italy cannot furnish them enough, nor such as will be useful in India as well as Europe. But we leave this point to those who best understand it.

The account we have of the Turkish conditions is somewhat imperfect as yet.

1st.——The Turks will yield all that is taken, with Belgrade, and their dependencies.

2d.——Restitution of slaves on both sides.

3d.——Four millions they will give in money. The Emperor asks much more.

4th.——They will give up Jerusalem and Bethlem to the Roman Catholic religious, they paying such tribute as the Greeks now pay.

5th.——To Poland they offer a sum of money only.

6th.——To the Venetians, Candia, and what they have conquered in Dalmatia; but what they will give to the Pope, besides the Holy Sepulchre, is not yet said.*

---

* These negotiations and conditions came to nothing, as the war continued with various success till the peace of Carlowitz, in 1699.

The Corn-meter that was reputed dead, proves to be alive, and in health, though the late Lord Mayor had disposed of his place in favour of his son.

For John Ellis, Esq. Secretary to the
   Commissioners for the Revenue of
   Ireland,   At Dublin.

CLXXX.

Trial of the Officers of the Duke of Berwick's Regiment.
—Mayor of Scarborough tossed in a blanket.—Foreign
news, &c.

London, Sept. 11th, 1688.

SIR,

THE Lieutenant-colonel and four Captains that refused to take in the Irishmen in the Duke of Berwick's regiment at Portsmouth, were tried yesterday at Windsor before a Council of War of General Field-officers. The fact seemed to be more favourable for the officers than was given out at first, all of them alleging that they knew nothing of those Irishmen

coming to town ; that the Duke of Berwick
had never spoken to them of incorporating
them in their companies ; that their companies
were complete, and no allowance for supernu-
meraries ; and that they did not mutiny against
or oppose any order, but had only written to
Major Slingsby to desire him to represent these
matters to the Duke. What resolution the
Council of War will come to we know not.*

* The account given by Burnet of this transaction is as
follows :—" A new and unlooked for accident gave the King a
very sensible trouble. It was resolved, as was told before, to
model the Army, and to begin with recruits from Ireland.
Upon which the English army would have become insensibly
an Irish one. The King made the first trial upon the Duke
of Berwick's regiment, which being already under an illegal †
Colonel, it might be supposed they were ready to submit to
every thing. Five Irishmen were ordered to be put into
every company of that regiment, which then lay at Portsmouth. But Beaumont, the Lieutenant-colonel, and five of
the Captains, refused to receive them. They said they had
raised their men upon the Duke of Monmouth's invasion, by
which their zeal for the King's service did evidently appear.
If the King would order any recruits, they doubted not but
that they should be able to make them. But they found it

† As a Roman Catholic.

Another complaint will suddenly be brought before them by the Mayor of Scarborough, who says he was tossed in a blanket by the command of Captain Waseley,* who quarters in that town. What provocation the Mayor gave is not said, but a messenger is sent to bring the Captain up in custody.

Yesterday there came an express from Flanders to the Spanish Ambassador, with the news of Belgrade's being taken by the Elector of

would give such an universal discontent, if they should receive the Irish among them, that it would put them out of a capacity of serving the King any more. But as the order was positive, so the Duke of Berwick was sent down to see it obeyed. Upon which they desired leave to lay down their commissions. The King was provoked by this to such a degree, that he could not govern his passion. The officers were put in arrest, and brought before a Council of War, where they were broken with reproach, and declared incapable to serve the King any more. But upon this occasion, the whole officers of the Army declared so great an unwillingness to mix with those of another nation and religion, that as no more attempts were made of this kind, so it was believed that this fixed the King in a point that was then under debate, namely, with regard to receiving succours from France."

* In a subsequent letter this name is spelled *Ouseley*.

Bavaria; but as the news came as the Ambassador was going for Windsor, so we know not for certain whether it was by storm or by capitulation, though most do affirm his Excellency said it was by storm.

The Turkish Ambassador was come as far as Belgrade, time enough to be eye-witness of its being taken, and had had the Emperor's pass to come up to Vienna with his proposals for a peace. He hath about a hundred persons in his train, and hath letters to the Emperor and his allies, which unnecessarily let them see that the Sultan is weary of the war.

There are said to be letters by the last French post from Lyons, which mention a courier's passing through that place with the Pope's confirmation of the Cardinal of Furstemberg; but it is certain the Vienna letters of the 2nd, new style, say positively the Pope hath sent his confirmation to Prince Clement, with an injunction therein to the Cardinal of Furstemberg, not to oppose him in taking quiet possession of the Electorate, upon pain and penalty of being deprived of all the dignities he already hath. How far the French understand this sort of canon-law, time will tell us.

It is given out in Holland, that the King of Sweden hath promised the Prince of Orange to come into the present alliance with his forces by sea and land, and that he hath above thirty ships of war ready to sail, though he may want seamen as well as other nations.

The seamen of England, and of other countries which flocked to the Dutch, begin to desert again, and come over hither faster than they went. They find themselves trapped by a little Dutch sophistry, being they are listed to serve at sea, and yet fancy they are to be employed by land-service, or, as occasion shall serve, at both sea and land; which double duty tarpaulins cannot dispense with.

What is writ about of a living in Magdalen College gift, that is presented to by Dr. Hough and the ejected Fellows, is a false report.

The Dutch Ambassador is said to have

assured the King, that his masters the States were much surprised at our sea-preparations, which gave them the chief occasion to arm ; and that the French Memorial lately given in heightens their apprehensions, and that they would be glad to know, whereto that strict alliance mentioned therein doth tend.

There lately appears from hand to hand a new pamphlet called *The Anatomy of an Equivalent,** which makes great noise, and is censured according to each man's passion : it is very sharp and biting, though the application be veiled over, and is said to be writ by a noble peer.

For John Ellis, Esq. Secretary to the
   Commissioners for the Revenue of
   Ireland,   At Dublin.

---

* " The Anatomy of an Equivalent," a political pamphlet of the day, long since forgotten, was written by George (Savile) Marquis of Halifax.

CLXXXI.

Queen of Portugal brought to bed.—Death of Lord Spencer.
—Various news.—Queen and Princess Anne reported to
be with child.

London, Sept. 13th, 1688.

SIR,

THE Queen-dowager had news out of
Portugal, that the Queen is brought to bed of
a Prince,* to the great joy of every body except the Infanta, who now will scarce have
those great matches that were once offered her,
and may not improbably be doomed to see
her beauty and youth wither within the walls
of a cloister.

On the 6th inst. died at Paris the Lord Spencer, eldest son of the Earl of Sunderland, Lord
President and Principal Secretary of State,
after a long and painful fit of sickness; the
first cause whereof is said to have been a wound

* Mary Elizabeth, daughter of the Elector Palatine, and
wife of Peter II. The son of which she had been just
brought to bed, died before the conclusion of the year 1688.

given him some years ago by a gentleman at Bury in Suffolk.

The D. of Lorraine is said to be very far advanced in the treaty with the Turks, who, seeing Fate (whom they trust much in) and Victory bent against them, will comply with any terms that are not very dishonourable and ruinous.

We cannot yet hear any farther particulars of the taking of Belgrade, than that it was by storm, and not by capitulation ; Yeghen Pacha having sworn by the beard of Mahomet, that, if they surrendered it, he would destroy all those the Elector should spare. The Elector of Bavaria is slightly wounded ; Count Staremberg, and some other of the briskest men, are killed.

It is again confirmed to us that Dr. Hough and the ejected Fellows of Magdalen College did present one Doctor Bayly, one of their own Fellows, to a living in the College gift, and that the person presented by Bishop Gifford and the present Fellows was rejected by the Bishop of Glocester.*

Some will needs pretend there is not any truth in what the Weekly Occurrencer writes, viz. that the Dissenters had offered to lend his Majesty a considerable sum of money. They allege that their practice in past times makes it now hard of belief, and very improbable; but the case is altered.

Another story there runs, how that a noble Peer,† lately reconciled to the Church of Rome, would have borrowed a sum of 10,000*l*. of a certain rich eminent lawyer, some days ago. The writings were said to be drawn, and all things agreed; but the lawyer happening to understand the Lord was reconciled, flew off again,

* Dr. Robert Frampton. He was deprived after the Revolution, for refusing to take the oaths. The living in question was in his diocese. Gifford, as has been before stated, was the Roman Catholic head of Magdalen College appointed by James after the death of Parker.

† I cannot make out who this peer was, unless Lord Sunderland, who had lately changed his religion, and who, from his extravagant habits, was always in want of money.

for that he could not take the security of one that had by the law incurred the penalty of his circumstances, and had no pardon for it.

The Queen is said to be with child again, and so also the Princess of Denmark.

The late Lord Mayor was buried the last night.

For John Ellis, Esq. Secretary to the
   Commissioners for the Revenue of
   Ireland,   At Dublin.

CLXXXII.

Memorials of French and English Envoys in Holland.

London, Sept. 14th, 1688.

SIR,

THOUGH the present conjuncture affords more than ordinary variety of news from abroad, yet the eyes and ears of all being fixed most upon the preparations now a-making in Holland, I will gratify the reader with the best account I have from the place, which is in two

Memorials given in to the States-General by the French Ambassador * and one of the English Envoys.

MY LORDS,

The sincere desire which the King my master has to maintain the peace of Europe, will not suffer him to see the great preparations which your Lordships make by sea and land without taking those measures which the prudence that accompanies all his actions inspires him with, for the preventing those mischiefs which these warlike preparations must draw after them.

And though the King is persuaded of the wisdom of your councils, and that it cannot be thought that a Republic can be so easily disposed to take arms, and to kindle a war that must be fatal to all Christendom, yet his Majesty cannot believe your Lordships will be at

* Burnet observes, in speaking of the Dutch preparations, "France took the alarm first, and gave it to the Court of England."

that charge within and without your provinces, that they would list soldiers and invite foreign troops, that they would equip so great a fleet so late in the year, and make such other great preparations, but that they have some design projected that is suitable to so vast an expense.

These, and other circumstances, make the King my master believe that this arming is designed against England; wherefore he has commanded me to declare to you, that the ties of friendship and allegiance with the King of Great Britain, will not only oblige him to succour him, but to look upon the first act of hostility which your troops or ships shall do against the King of England, as a manifest breach of the peace, and an open rupture against his own Crown.

I leave your Lordships to consider hereof, and of the consequences such an attempt may have; his Majesty having not ordered me to declare this to you, but out of that real desire

he hath to prevent any thing which may disturb the peace of Europe.

Given at the Hague, the 9th of Sept. 1688.

Signed,   COUNT D'AVAUX.*

MY LORDS,

The underwritten Ambassador has received orders from his King to tell your Lordships that, as he is informed of the motions of

* John Anthony de Mesmes, Count d'Avaux, was employed in various embassies during the reign of Lewis the
Fourteenth.   He died in 1709.   St. Simon gives the follow-
ng account of him. —" The Count d'Avaux was one of the
plenipotentiaries at Nimeguen, where, like a true courtier as
he was, he attached himself to Croissy, his colleague, the bro-
her of Colbert.   Some time after the peace of Nimeguen,
D'Avaux was Ambassador in Holland.   The name he bore
was of great use to him in the situations he filled, and persuaded him that he was as capable of filling them as his
uncle.†   It must, however, be allowed, that he was possessed
of talents, of address, of the art of insinuation, of good temper, and that, in fact, he was as able a man as his uncle.   He
was always well informed upon all political matters.   He ac-
quired the friendship and the consideration of the people in
Holland to a very singular degree."

† Claude de Mesmes, Count d'Avaux.

N 2

troops upon the frontiers of Cologne, in opposition to the Cardinal of Furstemberg and that
Chapter, so his Majesty is resolved to maintain the Cardinal in their rights and privileges
against all those that would disturb them therein : his Majesty assuring himself that those
that love the preservation of the public peace,
will do no hostile act against the said Cardinal and Chapter, nor against any place or
part of that Electorate, the government and
administration whereof belongs to them.
        Made at the Hague, Sept. 8th, 1688.
                Signed,   COUNT D'AVAUX.

MY LORDS,

        The great and surprising preparations
of war which your Lordships make by land
and sea, in a season when all operations of
war, especially by sea, usually cease, give just
occasion of surprise and alarm to all Europe,
and oblige the King my master, (who, since
his coming to the Crown, has had nothing
dearer to him than the keeping the general

peace, and a good correspondence with this State,) to order me, the Marquis d'Albyville, his Envoy-extraordinary with your Lordships, to require from them, upon what design the same are made. His Majesty, as being their ancient ally and confederate, thinks himself in the right to demand such a declaration, which he hoped to have had from their own Ambassador; but as he sees the *devoir* of alliance and confederation is delayed, and that your Lordships go on still to arm so powerfully without telling him the least thereof, his Majesty finds himself obliged to increase his fleet, and to put himself into a condition to maintain the peace of Christendom.

Hague, the 8th of Sept. 1688.

Signed, D'ALBYVILLE.

What answer will be given upon these three memorials time must tell us, when the States meet next week.

Belgrade holds out still, though the Elector of Bavaria spares no powder. The Duke* is

---

* Of Lorraine.

thought to be gone down to treat of peace, rather than to fight : some of the conditions proposed our next will give an account of.

Sir John Shorter, Lord Mayor, died this morning, and Sir Robert Viner some days since.

(No address on this Letter.)

CLXXXIII.

London, Sept. 15th, 1688.

SIR,

By the next Dutch post we may expect the answers of the States-General to the three Memorials given in at the Hague by the English and French Ministers there, touching the Dutch preparations. In the mean while, that newly arrived tells us that the Prince of Orange has been at Minden, a town in Westphalia belonging to the Elector of Brandenburgh, and is said to have been met by that Elector and some of the German Princes, as well as by the General Schomberg * and Prince Waldeck ;† some adding that he is declared Generalissimo of the Confederate forces upon the Rhine.

The armies to be now encamped are to lie in three several places : the Dutch, which are about 22,000, upon the heath of Nimeguen ; the Brandenburghers, which are about 20 or 16,000, in the land of Cleves ; and the German auxiliaries, which will make about 20 or 25,000 men, at or near Dusseldorf, beyond the Rhine, within six hours of Cologne.

We hear no more of the Dutch fleet, only that they sail before their own coast, and that they still are fitting out more ships to be sent out to sea.

The Dutch Ambassador arrived on Wednesday, and went straight to Court, where, no doubt, he hath ere this given his Majesty some account of his Masters arming in Holland.

* Afterwards Duke of Schomberg. Killed at the battle of the Boyne.

† Christian Lewis, Prince of Waldeck. A general of considerable ability. He was a Field-marshal in the service of the Emperor of Germany. He died December 21st, 1706.

At Portsmouth there happened some difference between the Duke of Berwick, whose regiment is there in garrison, and the captains and officers of the same. The occasion was this, that the Duke wanted some men to recruit his said regiment. But Colonel Mackillicott, who lately raised a regiment in Ireland, brought over forty or fifty above his number. These men were ordered to be received in the Duke of Berwick's regiment, which the Lieutenant-colonel (Mr. Beaumont) and five or six of the Captains refused; alleging they were raw undisciplined Irishmen, and that, if the regiment was to be recruited with raw men, they had all of them credit enough to raise Englishmen; and all of them signed a paper to that effect; which being sent to the King, his Majesty ordered them to be fetched in custody by a party of horse, and they are to be tried on Monday at a council of war. The Captains' names I know not; one is Captain Paston, brother to Lord Yarmouth,* another is called Cook, &c.

* William (Paston) second and last Earl of Yarmouth of that family.

The Queen-dowager thinks of going to live retiredly, and to receive no visits but from the Royal family.

We do not hear that the writs for Parliament are quite ready, but that strong interests are a-making in several parts of England and Wales.

For John Ellis, Esq. Secretary to the
   Commissioners for the Revenue of
   Ireland,   At Dublin.

CLXXXIV.

Indian News.—Canvassing for Elections in different places.—
Turkish and German News.

London, Sept. 15th, 1688.

SIR,

WE are told from Scotland, that the skirmishes which lately happened in the Highlands, between the two families, or clans, of the Macdonnels and the Mackintoshes, are now appeased by some of the forces of that kingdom, but that several have been killed on both sides. The first difference began about taking possession of certain lands which were decreed to the one in prejudice of the other.

The Lord Dartmouth is gone down the River to Chatham, and it is said his Majesty may be there about Tuesday next.

The Lord Chancellor hath been in town since Wednesday ; the Parliament writs are all ready, and will be sealed and delivered out next Tuesday.

The Royal African Company have lately a dividend of ten guineas per cent. We do not hear that the East India Company is about making any : Dr. St. Johns, who complains of their behaviour in India, hath petitioned his Majesty against them, and the Company are to give in their answer to it.

We hear of some other Englishmen that are arrived lately from the East Indies, who sing to the same tune with Dr. St. Johns ; and, among other particulars, say, that there were several Englishmen lately murdered by the King of Siam's subjects, who were provoked to it by the ill-usage of some of our Company in those parts.

Two nights ago, the Lord Dover's house in Albemarle Buildings was robbed, and a great quantity of plate taken.

We hear of great canvassings that are already in many counties and corporations; several new charters are now a-passing the Great Seals, in order to qualify those corporations the better to elect members for the ensuing Parliament.

Our Vienna letters newly arrived, confirm to us the taking of Belgrade by storm, after a vigorous defence; it having cost the Germans a great many brave men in the three repulses they met with in their general assault; among whom, of most note, are the Count of Scherffemberg, Count Emanuel of Furstemberg, and a Count Starremberg, son of the Mareschal-decamp of the same name, Governor of Vienna. This conquest is of the highest importance; it not only ascertains the reduction of all the strong places remaining in the Turks' hands; not only gives a passage into Servia and Misnia, Bulgaria and Romania; but has left nothing capable of stopping the Emperor himself, if he pleases, from going to take a taste of the *Serrail* at Constantinople.

The same letters advise us, that the Duke of Lorraine had been in the camp before Belgrade ; that he had drawn thence a great body of horse, and was gone to give chace to Yeghen Pacha's poor Mussulmen.   His Highness was to be joined by Count Dunewaldt and Prince L. of Baden,* who, besides the advantages formerly mentioned, has had a new victory over the Turks, killing 5000 upon the spot, taking 2000 prisoners, with all their baggage and cannon.

Lower Germany seems full of presage of an ensuing rupture.   For many ages have there not been known so many going and coming,

* Lewis William, Prince and Margrave of Baden, whose bravery and successes against the Turks have placed his name very high among those of great captains.   He was peculiarly celebrated for his manner of throwing up and defending intrenchments ; of which, perhaps, his *chef-d'œuvre* was the famous lines of Stolhofen.   He died, worn out with fatigues, at the age of fifty-two, January 4th, 1707; having made twenty-six campaigns, commanded at twenty-five sieges, and fought thirteen battles, in most of which he was successful.

nor so great a correspondence and harmony, as is seen at this day between the Electors and other Princes of the Empire and their allies. The Elector of Brandenburgh passed through Hanover in his way to Minden, where he hath conferred with the Elector of Saxony, the Dukes of Brunswick, and Lunenbourg, the Prince of Orange, the Landgrave of Hesse-Cassel, and some other Princes, as also with the Bishop of Munster at Cloppenburg: since which conferences, several of the Confederate troops are on their march; those of Zell and Wolfenbuttel began theirs on the 2d of September; and we also expect that our next Northern couriers should bring us notice of the Swedish fleet being put to sea. *

Our last Paris letters inform us, that they take the war there to be infallible, and that it will be the fiercest that has been in that King's reign, as well as of some continuance; they

---

* The Princes mentioned in the foregoing paragraph were mostly those who had agreed to assist the Prince of Orange in his designs with regard to England.

looking upon it as a war of religion, policy, and state.

Our Holland mails are wanting.

For John Ellis, Esq. Secretary to the
 Commissioners for the Revenue of
 Ireland, At Dublin.

CLXXXV.

Dutch fleet at sea.—Cabinet Council holding, and the King present at it.—State of Duke of Berwick's regiment.

London, Sept. 18th, 1688.

DEAR SIR,

YESTERDAY I met with Roguy Rene, who indeed acknowledges the debt for due, but pleads poverty; saith he had 75*l*. deducted by way of mistake that he had not been at his troop after the first signing his commission so soon as really he was, and Dom. Sheldon was in the same condition, and got it : he hath petitions, references, and reports thereupon, and it only stuck in the briars for want of due care and managery. This is his story, and he says Jack Price knows it, to whom he owes likewise ten pounds.   He offers this title in order to reimburse you both.   Pray speak with Price about it ; and if it is feasible, I will transmit you what he has to show for it : any other way I despair of doing good of him. I know you will not fail of doing what you may with Colonel Sarsefeild and Aunt Eustace. We are in great expectations still what will be the consequence of these great preparations of the Dutch : the French fleet and ours joined are not able to cope with them, and we want six thousand seamen of our complement ; that is, to make thirty-eight ships for fight, and twelve fire-ships.   The French have besieged Philipsburgh, which is the news to-night. The Circles of Germany have put 10,000 men into Cologne, and the Pope's declaration is in favour of the French King's interest for the Cardinal of Furstenberg.   The Dutch are seventy-six sail at sea, waiting hourly for their Northern fishers, to take the men, and then the design to be put in execution !   The King said yesterday, it was either an invasion upon France or us; but no man doubts upon which side the scale will fall. There are **10,000** landsmen on board, and accoutrements for **4000** horse. None can imagine, that does not see, how the general expectation is. I am now in Lord Sunderland's office, where a Cabinet Council is holding, the King in it; came from Windsor this evening on purpose, goes to-morrow to Chatham, then to Portsmouth, where matters are in mighty disorder: the subalterns, since Beaumont &c.'s cashiering, generally laid down, and many soldiers run away. Ben Fletcher has a company of one of those cashiered captains. The Prince of Orange says he will be aboard the fleet the **25**th, our style. They expect **6000** Swedes aboard them. I dare not say what the Declaration consists of, but it is the height of what can be imagined. The Prince and Princess are come from Tunbridge, and the Household removes from Windsor wholly on Thursday. I expect few days more of quiet, but am ready and determined.

Tho. Chudleigh and Constable are gone to be Carthusians.

For John Ellis, Esq. Secretary of His
   Majesty's Revenue in Ireland,
Ireland.   At Dublin.

———

CLXXXVI.

Bet between the Election of Bavaria and Duke of Mantua.—
Other Foreign news.—Movements of the Court, &c.

London, Sept. 18th, 1688.

SIR,

SINCE our last we have these farther particulars of the taking of Belgrade :—That the Duke of Bavaria had laid a wager of 10,000 pistoles with the Duke of Mantua,* that the place would be taken by such a day, and had his wager ; that the Duke of Lorraine

* Ferdinand Charles IV. Duke of Mantua, a foolish and profligate prince. He served in the Imperial armies, but without distinction, and even under considerable suspicions with regard to the common merit of courage. He died July 5th, 1708 ; it is said of poison, administered to him by a lady he was in love with.

VOL. II.   O

had been in the camp, and had dined (but, by agreement, was to stay no longer), and did not imagine the Elector would have given the assault so soon, which was another reason caused the Elector to make the greater haste ; that there were 9 or 10,000 Turks killed, and about 1200 Christians ; there were three or four of the chief officers killed ; and that the Elector had a slight glance of an arrow upon his right cheek.

Cardinal Furstemberg would not have been sorry the arrow had aimed better ; for by that means he might have been freed of his rival at Cologne, where the faggot seems ready to kindle ; the troops on both sides having taken their several stations till the Conclave at Rome gives the word of command, that is, till the Pope approves of one or other of the competitors.

Some letters thence say the Pope has found out nullities in the elections on both sides ; if so, that part of the world may live in peace a little longer, and the parties go to a new election, which the Cardinal will scarce be persuaded to, when he has eleven points of the law already on his side.

The French intend three armies of 40,000 each, to be commanded by the King, Dauphin, and Monsieur,* that King being inclined to give the world one instance more of his courage, and loth to lose so fair an opportunity as the making head against the united strength of the whole Empire.

If it be true that the French have already passed the Rhine, and that Cologne has renounced all neutrality, and is taking in a German garrison, we may conclude it will not be long ere it come to blows; the Allies being but four hours from them.

* Philip of France, Duke of Orleans, only brother of Lewis the Fourteenth; a weak, profligate, and effeminate prince, of whom his second wife, in her Memoirs, has left us some strange and very discreditable stories. He was, however, personally brave, much more so than his elder brother. When he was with the army, the soldiers used to say of him, " Monsieur craint plus que le soleil ne le hale, qu'il ne craint la poudre et le feu des mousquets."

The Dutch fleet is said, and believed by most people, to be between Dunkirk and England, about sixty or seventy sail strong, augmented by several Swedes men-of-war, but of this there is no certainty.

His Majesty goes down to Chatham to-morrow morning, and stays about three days. The Queen and Court remove from Windsor on Thursday, it having been resolved so on last Sunday night very unexpectedly.

There is an account from Portsmouth that some more officers of the D. of Berwick's regiment have laid down their commissions upon the same account with the other officers, that were lately cashiered ; and some will have it that several of the common soldiers run away and follow their officers, though they venture hanging by it.

Wasely, that tossed the Mayor of Scarborough in a blanket, is fled into Holland.

The D. of Ormond is chosen one of the Governors of the Charter-house, so that he had the good luck to succeed in all his grandfather's places, except the Stewardship of Winchester.

Last Sunday night Sir Robert Vyner was buried in St. Mary Woolnoth church, in Lombard-street.

Yesterday a regiment filed off from Tower-hill, and is said to be marched for Portsmouth.

For John Ellis, Esq. Secretary to the
Commissioners for the Revenue of
Ireland,   At Dublin.

CLXXXVII.

Arrival of the Court.—Dutch Fleet on the coast of Holland.—
Case of Mr. Skelton.—Foreign news.

London, September 20th, 1688.

SIR,

ON Monday night the Princess of Denmark came to Whitehall from Tunbridge, and on Tuesday came the King from Windsor, and this day her Majesty the Queen and Prince of Wales are expected.

Yesterday his Majesty went down the River to Chatham to view the ships that are there fitting out, which we are told are five, and three fire-ships, to be added to the fleet.

We hear no more of the Dutch fleet or of its design: our last letters of the 24th, left it upon the coast of Holland, cruising before the Maes: the report of its appearing upon our coast was a mistake, raised by our timorous oyster or herring-women, who are concerned for their trade.

On Tuesday night there was a Council held at Whitehall, where the case of Mr. Skelton,*

* " The French Ambassador at the Hague in a Memorial told the States, that his Master understood their design was against England ; and in that case he signified to them, that there was such a strict alliance between him and the King of England, that he would look on every thing done against England, as an invasion of his own crown. This put the King of England and his Ministers much out of countenance ; for, upon some surmises of alliance with France, they had very positively denied there was any such thing. Albeville did continue to deny it at the Hague, even after the Memorial was put in. The King did likewise deny it to the Dutch Ambassador at London ; and the blame of the putting it into his Majesty's Envoy at Paris, was taken into consideration : he had landed at Deal but the day before, and after Council on Tuesday, he was sent prisoner to the Tower. What his crime is we yet know not, but are told it is some false step he made to the Court of France, by meddling with what he had no instructions for, and by exceeding his commission ; the farther particulars whereof you may have hereafter.

The Dauphin is marched out of Paris with a numerous train of French nobility, and is gone towards Germany to command the King's army there, and to enter himself in the theatre

the Memorial was cast on Skelton, the King's Envoy at Paris, who was disowned in it, and upon his coming over, was put into the Tower for it. This was a short disgrace, for he was soon after made Lieutenant of the Tower. His rash folly might have procured the order from the Court of France to own this alliance. He thought it would terrify the States ; and so he pressed this officiously, which they easily granted. That related only to their owning it in so public a manner ; but this did clearly prove that such an alliance was made." This is Burnet's account of the transaction. For the Memorial alluded to, see Letter CLXXX.

of war by besieging Philipsburgh, or some other considerable place.

Cologne hath actually received a German garrison into it. Notwithstanding all the offers and endeavours of the French, they are said to have a design of camping some thousands of men on the other side of the Rhine, over against Cologne, to observe the motions of the Allies ; so that city will be in danger of being bombarded with great ease.

Mareschal Schomberg is to command the Confederate troops upon the Rhine.

The French have clapped up several Germans in the Bastile at Paris, by way of retortion,* for that the Emperor refused passage to several French that were at Vienna.

The Pope is to have received the reply of the Congregation deputed to examine the election at Cologne, among whom there were not above two or three of seventeen for the Cardinal of Furstemberg. The Pope has not yet

* " Retortion, the act of retorting."—Johnson.

issued out his Bull or Brevet of Confirmation, though the Germans press for it.

The Parliament writs were delivered yesterday.

For John Ellis, Esq. Secretary to the
Commissioners for the Revenue of
Ireland,   At Dublin.

CLXXXVIII.

The King sends for the Bishops.—Changes talked of.—Dutch
Fleet.—Successes of the French.

London, Sept. 21st, 1688.

SIR,

It pleaseth his Majesty to give every day some mark or other of his gracious intention to preserve the Church of England as established, and thinks fit to convince the Bishops of it in the first place; and in order to that, he has sent for several of them to come up to Court. Some already have attended on his Majesty, as the Lord Bishop of Ely* did last night, and all have been dismissed very well satisfied. The Archbishop and Bishop of London are expected to-day or to-morrow.

As for what the Coffee-man† writes, that the Earl of Rochester had kissed the King's hand on Sunday, it is only a piece of his own invention, the said noble Lord having appeared always at Court.

Several alterations in the present state of things are commonly talked of; as the restitution of Magdalen College fellows, the superseding of the Ecclesiastical Commission, &c. which a few days will tell us farther of.‡

* Thomas Watson, Bishop of Ely; deprived in 1699 for simony and other offences.

† This means the news-writer of the coffee-houses—the places, at this time, the most frequented by those who sought after news.

‡ "The King began now, though fatally too late, to be sensible of his error in carrying matters to so enormous a length at the instigation of Popish councils; and now restored several justices of the peace in most counties, as also the old charters all England over. He now quits his hold of the Bishop of London, does justice to Magdalen College, and begins again to court the Church of England."—Reresby's Memoirs.

Five-and-twenty companies are to be raised to be added to the several regiments ; we do not hear who the new officers are for the other new levies. Marquess de Miremont (the Earl of Feversham's nephew, and a Protestant,) is to be one.

We hear no more of the Dutch fleet, and have no certain account of the preparations or numbers that it hath, but are well assured that not a Swedish ship or man are joined to it, the Swedish fleet having only showed their sails in the air, and put back again into Calmer Sondt.

We have been in some apprehension as if the Dutch fleet designed their force against England. There are letters come from France which say, that the Court begins now to be sensible it is aimed against them, and as a diversion to them while they are disputing by land upon the Rhine.

The French King hath not yet resolved whether he may venture in person against Germany. But as the Dauphin is to open the trenches this day before Philipsburgh,* and thereby all the ties and treaties (which have kept all parties hitherto in peace) will be dissolved : so it is probable the P. of Orange will so order his first blow as to keep time with the French ; but as the season is advanced, and the moon in its strength, so a very few days will reveal this mystery, and tell us whether Great Britain, or little Bretagne be levelled against.

Several Dutch ships are arrested in France.

The French are said to have taken Keysers-Lauteren in the Palatinate, and to have turned out the Pope's vice-legate from Avignon ;† and that they are now marching to settle the Duke

* The Dauphin had under him the Marshal de Duras to command the troops, and the celebrated Vauban to direct the siege.   Philipsburgh, ill-defended by Stahremberg, capitulated on the 29th of October.

† Boufflers took Keyserlauter on the 20th of September. Lewis had seized upon Avignon as a reprisal upon the Pope, who had excommunicated his ambassador at Rome, the Marquis de Lavardin, on account of the quarrel with regard to the Franchises.

of Parma* in his Dukedoms of Castro and
Roncilione.

The French Advocate-general† has made

* The Duke of Parma at this time was Ranuccio II. the
son of Duke Odoard. It does not appear that the French
Government took any decided steps at this time to regain
for the Duke his Duchy of Castro and County of Ronciglione,
though they threatened a good deal upon the subject. They
had been wrested from him by Pope Innocent X. in consequence of the assassination of the Bishop of Castro, by command of the Duke's minister. This happened in 1649. In
1660, Cardinal Mazarin, then Prime Minister of France, be-
sought the Pope Alexander VII. to restore to the Duke of
Parma these territories. But Alexander, who hated the Cardinal and his master, and besides probably preferred keeping
Castro and Ronciglione in his own hands, instead of com-
plying with the request, declared in full Consistory the do-
mains in question reunited in perpetuity to the Apostolic
Chamber. After this, the Duke was never able to regain possession of them.

† Dionysius Talon.—" He proposed the convocation of a
Council ; and because the Pope had refused the Bulls, and by
that means left thirty-five cathedrals in France destitute of
pastors, he advised the re-establishment of the ancient usages,
and the returning to the Pragmatic Sanction for the regulation
of Ecclesiastical affairs, the Pope having violated the Concor-
dat."—The President Henault's "Abrégé Chronologique de
l'Histoire de France."

another speech against the conduct of the Pope, by way of appeal to the next Council legally called.

For John Ellis, Esq. Secretary to the
    Commissioners for the Revenue of
    Ireland,   At Dublin.

CLXXXIX.

Parliament returned.—Fears of the Ministers, &c.

London, Sept. 22nd, 1688.
DEAR MR. ELLIS,

I AM just arrived here from Tunbridge, where the journey has been very pleasant, but especially because it has perfectly recovered my Cousin Cook, who with all imaginable respect presents his humble service to you. I begin now to long to know my doom, which I presume is over by this time. I assure you, had the place been of much more value, I must have run the hazard of it for my Cousin's sake, and therefore am the less in pain for the success. Mr. Cullyford has promised me to write a letter of thanks to you for your care of me in my absence, and likewise to give you his acknowledgments for your protection and good counsel to Coddan, which business, to tell you the truth, vexeth him to the very soul. I spent the whole day with him yesterday, where we drank your health most heartily. He has been in Dorsetshire, and has secured his election ; but must make a second journey, if the Parliament goes on, which at present is a doubt, the writs being stopped, though sealed the 18th. Our army continues stubborn, and will not mix with the Irish. The prospect of a Parliament frights our grand Ministers, and makes them disown their hot counsels ; and it is believed the Church of England will be highly caressed out of hand. The noise of the French and Dutch landing, which has frighted us so much of late, is now over ; the French being engaged in a war which perhaps will out-live him. But what do I trouble myself with public news, when every post

brings so many gazettes *à la main?*   Dear Sir,
I hope this will find you preparing for London, and that your next will direct me in what
part of the world I shall be so happy to see
you, for I long for an opportunity to let you
know, by word of mouth, how much I am
your humble servant,

FRANCIS CAVE.

My duty to Mr. Strong.   The inclosed is
from the countryman who has the care of
his house at Tunbridge.   My service to all
friends ; and pray let Mr. Tayler know I want
an answer to my last.

 * To Mr. John . . . .
  at the Custo . . . .
   in D . . .

---

* The address to this letter is thus torn off in the original.

CXC.

King's Declaration.—Privy Councillors absent.—Various
rumours.

London, Sept. 22d, 1688.

SIR,

YESTERDAY, his Majesty was graciously
pleased to give one farther instance of his royal
care and concern for his people, by publishing
another Declaration in Council, which is in the
press, and whereof the heads are :

1st.——That the Parliament shall sit in November, though artifices are used to make the
world believe the contrary.

2d.——That as his Majesty purposeth a legal
establishment of universal Liberty of Conscience, so he will preserve inviolably the Church
of England.

3d.——That the several Acts of Uniformity
shall be confirmed in all their clauses, except
those that inflict penalties.

4th.——That his Majesty is willing that Ro-
nan Catholics remain incapable of being mem-

bers of the House of Commons, that they may engross no share of the legislative power.

5th.—His Majesty will do any thing else that becomes a King, that is careful of the safety and advantages of his subjects ; and exhorts them to make choice of such Representatives as are of abilities and temper becoming such a trust.

6th.—All persons concerned to see the execution of any writs or precepts for elections, are to cause due publication thereof, that the members chosen be fairly returned, according to the true merits of their choice.

In opposition to his Majesty's Royal Declaration and intention, some coffee-house scribblers that skulk within the rules of Gray's Inn and Alsatia,* publish that the writs for the Parliament are stopped : which is a piece of falsehood, such as they deal in ; for the writs were actually delivered out to the Lords Lieutenants on Thursday last.

* The district of Whitefriars near the Temple, and the great resort of sharpers, and " of men who lived by their wits," as was then the phrase.

Another of their shams is that Mr. Penne* is made Comptroller of Excise arising from tea and coffee: which is also false, though one might think they might be better informed in matters relating to their own trade.

We have also another piece of these coffee-men's news, which is, that the Dutch Ambassador has lately put in a brisk Memorial to his Majesty: of which there is no certainty, as I am credibly informed.

It was expected that several Lords would have yesterday appeared in Council, which did not, as the Archbishop of Canterbury, Marquis of Halifax, etc. and that some new Privy Councillors would have been made, as the Bishops of Winchester† and Ely: the first having had

---

* William Penn, the Quaker.

† Dr. Peter Mews, translated in 1684 from the Bishopric of Bath and Wells. "He had been a Captain during the wars, and had been Middleton's Secretary, when he was sent to command the Insurrection that the Highlanders of Scotland made for the King in fifty-three. After that he came into orders: And though he knew very little of Divinity, or of any other learning, and was weak to a childish degree,

the honour to be long with the King in his closet, yesterday morning.*

Mr. Skelton is still in the Tower, and is in more danger than was at first apprehended.

We hear no farther of the Dutch fleet.

Captain Ousely is said to be come to town to give his reasons for tossing the Mayor of Scarborough in a blanket. As a part of his plea, he has brought with him a collection of articles

yet obsequiousness and zeal raised him through several steps to this great see."—Burnet.

* The vacillations of the King backwards and forwards, as either his fears of the Dutch or his bigotry predominated, were most injurious to him at this time, and naturally gave occasion to the contradictory reports which are mentioned in this letter. As a proof of his unsettled will, the following passages of Lord Clarendon's Diary are curious. "Sept. 24th (1688,) I visited my Lord Chancellor, who told me that on Saturday last the King was resolved to call all the peers together, who were in and about the town, to consult with them upon the present state of affairs; that he would set all things upon the foot they were at his coming to the Crown; that in order thereto, his Majesty had commanded him to restore all the old honest Aldermen of the city, who had been turned out."—" Sept. 27th. I went to the Chancellor's: he told me all was nought; some rogues had changed the King's mind; that the Virgin Mary was to do all."

against the said Mayor, and the attestations of many gentlemen of note.

For John Ellis, Esq. Secretary to the
Commissioners for the Revenue of
Ireland,   At Dublin.

CXCI.

News-writer cudgelled.—General Pardon.—Foreign news.
—City Address to the King.—Duke of Albemarle.

London, Sept. 25th, 1688.

SIR,

IN the last were mentioned some coffee-house news-writers who make it their business to poison the town and country with their false news. One of them has since been met with by a gentleman whom he had scandalized in his newspaper, and was lustily convinced by cudgel argument, in the presence of many good witnesses, that he was in the wrong. Several others wait an opportunity to thresh his jacket in the same manner, which is the least could be expected by people that venture so far beyond their province, in matters too which require so much niceness, penetration, and judgment.

The seven officers of the Duke of Berwick's regiment that delivered up their commissions were dismissed on Saturday, without being tried by a Court-martial.

His Majesty being desirous to heal the faults as well as animosities of his subjects, by all the ways he can, is graciously pleased to grant another general pardon for his subjects, some few of the most notorious excepted; which is now a-preparing.

Our last French letters brought two large Declarations of that King's; the one is against the Pope, wherein he blames his ill conduct against the Crown of France, and threatens to send his troops into Italy to take possession of Castro, Roncilione, and Avignon, till the Duke of Parma be restored and satisfied in virtue of the Treaty of Pisa, whereof the French King is guarand. The other paper is against the Emperor " and Empire, Elector Palatine and others," which he calls " his reason for retaking up of arms, and for persuading all Christendom of the sincerity of his intentions to preserve the general peace."*

" In the first paper it is said that the Pope's conduct has given occasion to the boldness of the Prince of Orange to form a design of invading England, of stirring the English subjects to a revolt, and of treating the birth of the Prince of Wales as supposititious, &c."

What effect, or what answer, these Declarations may have, time must tell us.

The Dutch letters say that they were much divided there between surprise and joy at his Majesty's Declaration to the Dutch Ambassador here, viz. that his Majesty had no alliance with France, whatever the French Ambassador's Memorial said to the contrary, and that he was resolved to maintain the public peace only, and not to engage in any war.

* " This Declaration was much censured, both for the matter and for the style. It had not the air of greatness which became crowned heads. The Duchess of Orleans' pretensions to old furniture was a strange rise to a war," &c.—Burnet.

His Majesty has thought fit to declare, he thought it necessary at this time to raise some few more forces, horse and foot, for the recruiting of his army.

Yesterday the Lord Mayor and Aldermen waited on the King and Queen to pay their duty upon their Majesties' return from Windsor. His Majesty, in his gracious return to the compliment, took notice of the report as if the Dutch intended to attempt upon England, and bid them not be concerned; that he would stand ror them, as his Majesty hoped they would stand for him; and as he had often ventured his person heretofore in defence of the Monarchy, so would he go as far as any body to do it still against any body that should offer to disturb our quiet; or to that effect; which renders all the men in the city both hearty and unanimous.

Besides the taking of Negropont, we are told that all the parts about, as well as the city and Government of Damascus, are revolted.

Elector of Bavaria, as we said, won 10,000 ducats from the Duke of Mantua, and gave hem to those that were most forward to follow him up the walls of Belgrade.

The Turkish Ambassador is said to have but half instructions for to conclude a peace.

The boors about Cologne attacked the Cardinal's* coach, but he happened not to be in it.

Two ships more are lately sent by the Adventurers upon the Spanish wreck, to go on where Sir John Narborough left. His Majesty has given a new grant of that and other wrecks for a year longer to the Duke of Albemarle, in consideration of his Grace's good service, being said to have exceeded his predecessors at Jamaica in good luck, as well as good conduct; being, as we are informed, about discovering a rich vein of silver in that plantation. This being the Queen's birth-day was solemnized with great joy, balls, ringing of bells, &c. The King of Poland† is said again to be dead.

For John Ellis, Esq. Secretary to the
    Commissioners for the Revenue of
    Ireland,   At Dublin.

* The Cardinal Furstemberg.
† John Sobieski.——He lived till the 17th of June, 1696, when he was carried off by an attack of apoplexy.

CXCII.

Sept. 27th, 1688.

WE are told by express this morning, that the Prince of Orange is to embark on board his mighty fleet for England, to-morrow, or on Monday next at farthest: this puts us into great hurry and confusion, all preparing for a brush;* and it is to be feared, his Majesty (whom God preserve!) will venture his own royal person.   Many of our nobility are said to be already with the Prince.

For John Ellis, Esq. Secretary for
  the Revenue of Ireland,
              At Dublin.

----

* " Sept. 24th. I went to the King's levee; and met his Majesty going to the Queen's side.   He told me the Dutch were now coming to invade England in good earnest.   I presumed to ask if he really believed it?   To which the King replied with warmth, ' Do I see you, my Lord?'   And then he said that an express arrived the last night with an account that two thousand men were already shipped off, and seven thousand more were marching to the sea-side.   ' And now, my Lord,' said he, ' I shall see what the Church of England-men will do.'   I answered, ' And your Majesty will

CXCIII.

Church of England more in favour than formerly.—Writs for the Parliament stopped.—Private affairs.

Custom-house, London, 27th Sept., 1688.
HONEST MR. ELLIS,

AFTER I have begged pardon for my long silence, which I do by this paper most heartily, I could not omit acquainting you that for certain my Lord Duke of Ormond has now his grandfather's Garter : and the public prints will show you that all the Deputy Lieutenants, and Justices of the Peace, that were lately laid aside, are ordered to be restored again : and things look with more favour toward the Church of England than formerly. All our great ministers' heads are full of the public affairs, we having every day more and more apprehensions of the Dutch and Prince of Orange's landing a powerful army for this kingdom, and having at the same time a great

see they will behave themselves like honest men ; though they have been somewhat severely used of late.' " Diary of Henry Earl of Clarendon.

fleet at sea. All preparations are a-making to oppose them both at sea and land; and the King has told the City he will meet them in person at the head of his forces, as soon as he hears of their landing. You may easily imagine the confusion all good people are in. I pray God preserve the King! I am just now told the writs for election of the Parliament are by order stopped or superseded in the Sheriffs' hands, and that they will not meet at the prefixed time. And so much I think I may venture to acquaint you, for you know it is out of my post to write news.

I must not forget to thank you for all kindnesses, and amongst them, more particularly for your friendship to poor Coddon, who I think is persecuted most unchristianly by Mr. Strong, and does not show him to be either so good a man or so good a Christian as I took him to be; but I hope now Mr. Dickinson is arrived with you, he will see him have justice, which is all I will ask of my friends for him, for, did I not know and believe him to be an honest man and good officer, I would not open my lips for him. I understood Mr. Strong has a design to bring Desmaneeres in his place, and remove Coddon to his ; but I had much rather he should be dismissed, if he cannot justify himself, than go hither to reconcile, or qualify the gentleman's unjust indignation. I have spoke and wrote to Mr. Dickinson, and Mr. Trynder, and Plowden for him ; and old Welsh Ale has given me his promise to serve him, which, between you and me, I do not believe, but would, for a certain reason, know how he does carry himself in this matter. I have troubled you too much, and therefore ask your pardon. My service to all that are so kind to ask for me ; among them, I am sure Will. Smith will not forget me, therefore hearty service to him and his little woman, and poor Lord Longford. All friends here are well ; Frank Cave dined with me to-day, and we drank your healths heartily ; put in a word in season in his favour, that his name be not

left out of the book of life. I am, with un-
feigned respect,

Sir,

Your very affectionate,

Faithful, humble Servant,

WILL. CULLIFORD.*

(No address on this letter.)

CXCIV.

State of the Fleet.—King's Proclamation.—The Bishops.—
Mayor of Scarborough's business.

London, Sept. 29th, 1688.

SIR,

THE Lord Dartmouth has been to view
the condition of the fleet, and is come back

* Mr. Culliford had been one of the Commissioners of Irish
Revenue, and was now a Commissioner of Customs in England.   He was an adherent of Hyde Lord Rochester.   There
is frequent allusion made to him in this Correspondence, and
also in the Letters of Henry Lord Clarendon.

again, but is to go down this next week in order to stay on board and command in chief in this expedition against the Dutch.

The last expresses come from Holland say, that the Prince of Orange was to embark on board their fleet, either the latter end of this, or beginning of next week ; and some report as if the Princess of Orange also was to come along with them.

His Majesty last night in Council was pleased to order a proclamation to be published touching the intended invasion of the Dutch, whereby he animates all his loving subjects to behave themselves like true Englishmen, and that they be neither daunted with Dutch prowess, (for the sake of the reputation of English courage,) nor suffer themselves to be carried away with those specious pretexts and insinuations which they intend to publish in their Declaration, whensoever it be scattered abroad. What ought to incite our courage against them the more is, that they are said to have one thousand Saxon horse on board, as if Old England were to be conquered a second time by that nation.

The writs of Parliament are to be recalled, and the elections to be put off, by reason of this unforeseen incident of an invasion.

His Majesty has ordered a body of instructions to be published for the regulating of the Flag, and of the salutes due to his Majesty at sea, the better to secure the rights of the Crown, which our neighbours, and the enemies of this kingdom, have so much envied, and so oft invaded.

The Bishop of London could not be found, being gone, it is thought, to his sisters in Yorkshire; but his suspension is taken off. The Archbishop was also indisposed, and could not wait on the King; but about ten others of the Bishops have attended his Majesty yesterday, and having been a long time in his closet, were dismissed very well satisfied, and one of the chief of them telling his friends that, *Omnia benè.* *

The Dukes of Ormond and Berwick have the Garters, and were invested therewith yesterday at a Chapter held on purpose at Whitehall.

The Mayor of Scarborough, and Captain Wasely, who tossed the other in a blanket, were heard last night before the Council. The Captain pleaded his Majesty's gracious general

---

* " Sept. 28th. Several of the Bishops are this morning with the King. I was told he expressed himself very graciously to them ; but spoke only in general terms, that it was not now seasonable to enter into particular disputes; that they should every day find more and more effects of his Majesty's kindness ; that he had given order for restoring the Bishop of London. The Archbishop was indisposed, and so could not come over the water. The Bishops of London and Bristol are not yet come to town, though both had been sent for. As the Bishops came from the King, several people in the rooms, as they passed, asked them how things went ? The Bishop of Winton, poor man ! answered, ' *Omnia bene.*' " —Diary of Henry Earl of Clarendon. The Bishop of Winchester was a remarkably weak and foolish man.—See note to the 190th Letter.

pardon, which is in the press, and so both were dismissed.

For John Ellis, Esq. Secretary to the
    Commissioners for the Revenue of
    Ireland,   At Dublin.

CXCV.

The King retraces his steps.—Rumours respecting the Dutch
fleet : and great consternation in England.

London, Sept. 29th, 1688.

DEAR SIR,

    I HAD yours of the 15th last night ; was sorry you stood in need of a secretary, but hope that misfortune wears off.   I doubt not but you are very desirous to hear how matters go here.   I went this day sevennight to Cashiobury,* and designed to stay till I heard tidings of the Dutch landing ; but I thought an alarm from my Lady Sunderland† was enough, so I returned on Thursday, found the King had called our Bishops, and yesterday gave strong

* The seat of Lord Essex.
† Anne Digby, wife of Robert Earl of Sunderland.

assurances of supporting the Church of England; restored the Bishop of London, declared for the re-admission of the secluded members of Magdalen College, and that he would break the Ecclesiastical Commission, and lay his dispensing power to be determined by the arbitrement of Parliament, which should immediately be called, and the corporations restored to their former tenure. These are strange things, but like all to prove true. I believe your Earl Tyrconnel is sent for this post, and Earl Granard made Chief Governor for the present, but your friend Clarendon returns. His brother Rochester will have our old Duke's* white staff; the young one had the Garter yesterday, and D. Berwick the other vacancy. The Dutch cannot sail before next Friday, according to the advices of last night, but I think they will come sooner. Earl Shrewsbury† is

---

* The Duke of Ormonde. His Staff means that of the office of Lord Steward of the Household.
† Lord Shrewsbury was now in Holland with the Prince of Orange.

thought in command there, but it is uncertain.
Most of our noblemen are out of town, which
looks odd. I am his Grace of Ormond's vo-
lunteer. Mr. Charles* came on Thursday from
travel, comes in for his snack in this bustle.
Abundance of commissions are out. We shall
face the enemy with 5000 horse and 20,000
foot; we think the Prince comes with no more
than 12,000 foot and 3000 German horse. I saw
Suffolk gentlemen Wednesday come up alarmed : the Holland packet told them the Dutch
were seventy-six great men of war, and had
a hundred tenders, which seemed full of foot
and horse. I know his first provision was for
30,000 men's transportation. Mr. H. Sydney,
Admiral Herbert,† and Lord Mordaunt, are
generally thought in command. I think we
shall be in motion about the 10th of the following month. The King is coining guineas for
the army to carry along ; hath settled the train

* Charles Butler, younger brother of the second Duke of
Ormonde ; created by King William, Earl of Arran. He was
at this time only seventeen years of age.

† Admiral Herbert commanded the Dutch fleet.

of artillery ; resolves to go in person, send the Queen, young Prince, and Princess of Denmark, to Portsmouth, and take Prince George with him. Dr. Wynn, I suppose, will send you the Declaration. All is panic here. You will be sure to hear of me, till I am knocked on the head.

For John Ellis, Esq. Secretary of His
    Majesty's Revenue in Ireland,
Ireland.   Dublin.

CXCVI.

John Ellis's arm broke.—Expectations of Invasion, &c.

2nd October, 1688.

DEAR SIR,

I DINED this day at James Clarke's, where some Irish friends of his came in, and surprised us with the very ill news that you had broke one of your arms with a fall from your horse. I was the more concerned at it, being in hopes to see you here suddenly. I assure you, you have very few friends in any part of the world that can be more troubled for any thing of misfortune that happens to you than myself. We are all here in great hurry, and in hourly expectation of an invasion, upon what grounds nobody yet knows; but mighty preparations of all kinds are making, and the wind hath been fair all day (if any thing can be fair that brings an enemy upon us) to bring the Dutch hither. I heartily wish you well put together again, and shall always be,

> Dear Sir,
>
> Your most affectionate servant,
>
> WM. SHAW.

Mr. J. Ellis.

For John Ellis, Esq. Secretary to the Commissioners of His Majesty's Revenues of Ireland,   Dublin.

CXCVII.

City Charter restored.

> Whitehall, 2nd Oct. 1688.

SIR,

    THIS evening his Majesty called before him in Council the present Lord Mayor and

Aldermen of London, as also those that were Aldermen at the time that judgment was entered against the City charter; and as a mark of his confidence in the loyalty and affection of the City (especially at this time that the nation is threatened by a foreign invasion), was graciously pleased to restore to the City its charter in the same terms they had it before, to the inexpressible surprise as well as joy of them all. His Majesty told them likewise that he thought the Dutch fleet was at this time under sail.

For John Ellis, Esq. Secretary for
   the Revenue, at Dublin,
      Ireland.

CXCVIII.

Reports concerning the Dutch armament.—King to command his troops in person.—Monmouthians missing, &c.

London, Oct. 2nd, 1688.
SIR,

THE advices from Holland continue to give us the same account of the Dutch fleet, that it lies, as (the Gazette has it) off of Goree, and is three or four hundred sail strong in capital men of war, and bylanders* for the transportation of troops. Their army is said to be about eighteen or twenty thousand strong, made up of High and Low Dutch, of refuged Frenchmen, English fugitives and rebels, and such like medley. Earl Maxfield,† they say, is to command all the horse, and Colonel Sidney the foot; and our late Admiral Herbert the fleet, and if fame be true, is to carry the Standard of England. According to the Dutch computation, this army will have conquered England, Scotland and Ireland, in six weeks' time; and so far are they from making any secret of it, that they make it their public brags, and is the common talk and vapouring of their carmen and fishermen about their streets; but we hope they reckon without their host, and that England and its old renown is not yet sunk so low, as to be made a prey to such mongrel invaders.

* Transports.   † Macclesfield.

We hear that many noblemen and others have prayed and had his Majesty's commission to raise men in their country for the public defence.

His Majesty is said to have resolved to march in his own royal person, (whom God preserve!) as soon as they are landed; and all the Court and his Ministers are preparing to attend him.

The Lord Bishop of Winchester is also ready to attend his Majesty, as he did against the rebels in the West.

Several of the Monmouthians that were pardoned after the Western rebellion, are said to be missing now; whence we may reasonably conclude, from the immutability of some men's tempers, they are slipped over for a new command upon this occasion.

The City is unanimously resolved for the common defence, and the London apprentices seem eager for an opportunity to try their loyalty and briskness against those new pretended invaders.

The Lord Dartmouth is gone down the River to hasten the fleet together, but will be back once again before they sail.

The Mayor of Cambridge (though once a Quaker) has taken the oaths from the Vice-Chancellor; but the Mayor of Oxford seems unwilling to do it.

For John Ellis, Esq. Secretary to the
   Commissioners for the Revenue of
   Ireland,   At Dublin.

CXCIX.

Reports from Holland. — Bankers broke.—Confusion in the City, &c.

London, Oct. 2d, 1688.

I APPREHEND this will be the last I shall write to you from hence for some time, the wind having been fair all night and to-day from Holland. Our Admiral is gone on board, and weighed anchor, with order to attend the Dutch wherever they go. The King will up with his standard and march upon the first tidings of their landing. The City of London had their old Charter promised this evening, and great help is hoped from them, as the reward of such a favour. It was time; for Lombard-street stared yesterday, Moor and Thomas[*] having given way, viz. shut up, and all their shops have been crammed this four days, and the merchants' accounts all agree in an invasion. Great confusion, all our noblemen out of town, and in uncertainty where they are. What I wrote on Saturday to you, was real measures taken, though most since retracted; but ere the next Saturday, I think all will again be made good.

For John Ellis, Esq. Secretary of His
    Majesty's Revenue in Ireland,
Ireland.   Dublin.

---

[*] Two of the Bankers, or "Goldsmiths," as they were called at this time.

CC.

Proofs of the Prince of Wales's birth.—Prince of Orange's Declaration.—Last news of the Dutch fleet.—Disgrace of Lord Sunderland.

London, 3d Oct. 1688.

SIR,

I HAVE yours, and kindly thank you for your many assurances of friendship to me and my friends. Inclosed I have sent you the King's speech, and proofs taken at Council concerning the Prince of Wales, which came out last night;* as also the Proclamation concerning the dispersing of the Prince of Orange's Declaration, which came forth just now, and was

---

* This was a very foolish proceeding on the part of James ; for, as Rapin observes, "Before this examination, the presumption of law was for the Prince, since he was owned by both parents, so that the proof lay on the other side, and ought to be offered by those that questioned it. But after the King had undertaken to prove the reality of his son's birth, by forty witnesses, of which more than thirty said nothing material, and the rest fixed no time to what they deposed, he left room to his enemies to object against those very depositions."

hiefly occasioned from the late apprehending
f one Capt. Lenou, that lately came from Hol-
and, with whom were seized several of them,
nd he committed to the gaol of Newgate,
nd will be tried the next week at the King's
3ench bar. Inclosed I have also sent you the
ast news of the Dutch fleet, which is supposed
o be sailed northwards; and we expect every
iour to have an account of their landing either
it Burlington-bay or in Scotland. Our fleet
s now at the Galloper off of Harwich. The
vind has been this four or five days at north
ind north-east. Pray acquaint Mr. Dickenson
ierewith; I having not time to write him.
My service to yourself and him, and all friends.
presume it is no news to you that the mighty
3underland is fallen,* but for what, is not

* Lord Preston succeeded him as Secretary of State. "It
s believed," says Rapin, "that his neglect of Skelton's let-
ers to him was the real cause of his disgrace. He said upon
his subject, 'If he gave no account of those letters to the
King, it was because Skelton never wrote but second-hand
iews.' But these were not mere letters of news. One

known; though, negatively, it is not for holding correspondence with the Dutch, as the
King declared in Council, but for other private
reasons best known to himself. As for poor
Coddan, who, I understand, is coming for England, he was forced to leave Cork to avoid the
oppression of the merchants, &c. let loose on
him. I wish you could prevail with Mr. Dickenson, &c. to give him a certificate of his service done in Ireland, and send the same to me,
with your character of him, which will be of
service to him; for I have still a mind to do
him all the good I can. And it will be of
mighty use to me, not to send him back to you,

Wickstead, formerly a monk, seized for holding correspondence with the King's enemies, charged the Earl of Sunderland to his face, with revealing his Majesty's secrets to the
Prince of Orange."—" It is certain, that though the Earl of
Sunderland embraced the Popish religion, he was, and still
is, suspected by the Papists. There are even Protestants,
who, owning that he betrayed his master, count this pretended
treachery an honour to him, since it tended to the good of
the kingdom."—Rapin's History, vol. ii.

but in order to provide for him here. I am, with all real and sincere respect,

Your's,

WILL. CULLIFORD.

Pray do me the favour to take care of the two letters inclosed.

For John Ellis, Esq. Secretary to the Hon. Commissioners of His Majesty's Revenue of Ireland at the Custom-House   In Dublin.

CCI.

Dutch troops on board.—The mob destroy the Mass-houses.

London, Oct. 9th, 1688.

THERE was no news on Saturday, and not much now, only the packet that left the Brill on Saturday sevennight, and busked * at sea till last Saturday, says they were all on board, but the P. of Orange. Schomberg is

* " To busk," says Johnson, " is to make ready."

undoubtedly there.   Herbert wears a flag : nothing but the wind keeps them in, and, I believe, us from hearing of them, though you seem not convinced. They are surely much damnified by the hardness of these winds. The City is already making use of their new Charter ; and the rabble demolished the Mass-houses on Sunday, which is not taken notice of at Court.

For John Ellis, Esq. Secretary of His
    Majesty's Revenue of Ireland,
Ireland.   Dublin.

CCII.

Preparations for defence.—Successes of the French.—Coffee-houses suppressed.

London, Oct. 9th, 1688.

SIR,

WE are still in the dark in great measure as to the Dutch fleet, our last Holland letters being of the 28th past, which say that the Prince's Guards, and the rest of the Horse, were to be embarked the 1st and 2d instant, and he himself to come away the last week ; but the weather has been so bad, and the winds so cross, that it is not probable that they stirred all last week.

We hope that their delay does much good to, and in no wise prejudice to his Majesty's service : all England having time to be made the more sensible of the danger that threatens us ; and upon that account about 2000 Yorkshire gentlemen have listed themselves for the common defence, to be ready whenever they are called for by the Duke of Newcastle,* their Lord Lieutenant. The same is a-doing in other counties, all men being aware that every invader ought to be opposed (whatever his specious pretexts be). And this irruption that menaces

* Henry (Cavendish) second and last Duke of Newcastle of that family. He had been lately appointed Lord Lieutenant of the three ridings of Yorkshire, in the room of Lord Thomas Howard and Lord Fairfax, both Roman Catholics, at the request and representation of the gentlemen of the county.—See Reresby's Memoirs for the account of this transaction.

us from Holland is made up of French, Germans, Suisses, as well as Hollanders, who have all of them given large instances of their barbarity, as often as they have succeeded in their attempts.

A number of noblemen, knights, and gentlemen, are said to be also listing themselves under the D. of Ormond as their captain, each person to have four or five servants, well armed, to attend him.

If it be true that they put to sea last week, we may well hope they are already sick of their enterprise, it having been one continual storm, as it was also yesterday.

While the Dutch pretend to make conquests in England, we hear the French have taken eight or ten places upon the Rhine, within the Palatinate ; and have but Philipsburgh, (which is not like to hold out long,) and Francfort, and very few other strong places, to oppose them in those parts.

They have cast several bridges of boats over the Rhine, as if ~they had a mind to pour

French over that stream into the empire, and to master that whole river.

Yesterday the Lord Chancellor, by the King's command, directed the Justices of Peace of Middlesex to suppress all coffee-houses and other public houses that deal in news-letters, or expose to the public any foreign or domestic newspapers besides the printed Gazette. *

For John Ellis, Esq. Secretary to the
    Commissioners for the Revenue of
    Ireland,   At Dublin.

---

* This was a curious proceeding of Jefferies and his master, at a moment when they were anxious to make themselves popular, and when it was peculiarly important for them to show respect for the liberties of the subject.

CCIII.

Aldermen of London restored ; also the Fellows of Magdalen College.—The King exercises his troops.—Reports from Philipsburgh.

London, Oct. 11th, 1688.

SIR,

HAVING no letters from abroad since those dated the 30th past, we have no farther account as yet to give of our neighbours' design. The wind has been somewhat contrary to them these ten days, which may be one good reason why we have not heard from them.

Yesterday Sir John Chapman sat at the Old Bayly as Lord Mayor, and the old set of Aldermen, where there was great appearance ; and joy shined in all their looks, that they were met together, by his Majesty's grace and favour, contrary to all their expectations.

This day the Common Hall of the City met to choose the Lord Mayor and Sheriffs for the ensuing year, pursuant to their old charter ; and they have accordingly elected

Sir John Chapman Lord Mayor, Sir Humphry Edwynne and Mr. Fleet, Sheriffs. The late Chamberlain, Mr. Henry Roades, was displaced, and Sir Peter Rich restored to that employ, and the two Bridge Masters restored.

A detachment of 2 or 3000 men are to be sent hither from the Guards and troops in Ireland, to serve for this present imminent occasion, and then to return back again. Some part is already landed at Chester.

His Majesty having been graciously pleased to alter the present state of Magdalen College in Oxford, and to restore it to the last foundation-men, Bishop Gifford, the new President, is come up for London with his society, and the Lord Bishop of Winchester (who is the Visitor of the College) is gone down to re-establish the old Fellows.

We hear that that and the other University are a-consulting to raise some troops of Horse to serve his Majesty upon the present occasion at their own charges, as they did in Monmouth's rebellion in the West.

His Majesty sees his four troops of Guards frequently exercise in Hyde-Park in their armour, which they do to his satisfaction. Two of the gentlemen of which forces, discoursing about the proof and sufficiency of their armour, as they were defiling home, resolved to try each other's breast-pieces, and discharged their musketoons at each other's breasts, the armour answering the wished end, and receiving the bullet without yielding in the least.

A report is got into the City as if the Dauphin had been disturbed in the siege of Philipsburgh by the Elector of Saxony,* and that he was forced to raise the siege, and to swim for his life; which is the less probable, in that we have no fresh letters from those parts, and may well be interpreted to be a sham to amuse the people.

The Commissions of the Peace are a-renew-

* The Elector of Saxony, at this time, was John George the Third, born in 1647, died in 1691, while commanding the Imperial Army on the Rhine. The report mentioned in the text was a false one.

ing for the several counties of England, whereby the Church of England Justices are restored. The same will be done as to the Militia.

In the mean while our City Trained Bands are again on foot, and a company of the Orange Regiment had the honour of first mounting the guard at the Change on Tuesday night.

For John Ellis, Esq. Secretary to the
   Commissioners for the Revenue of
   Ireland,   At Dublin.

CCIV.

Imprisonment of Hubert Bourke and of Goodwin Wharton.—The Bishops ordered to prepare Prayers, &c.—Dutch Fleet kept back by contrary winds.

London, Oct. 13th, 1688.

SIR,

It is very certain that the Bishop of Winchester has received orders from his Majesty to repair to Oxford to establish Magdalen College there according to its ancient laws and statutes, and to restore Dr. Hough, the President, with the rest of the former society, and to expel the members that are now settled in that College.

One Hubert Bourke, one of the Evidence and Narrative-men in the late Popish plot, being lately come from Holland, where he pretended to have quitted a considerable employment to come to serve his Majesty, having, by his behaviour and language, given occasion to suspect the honesty of his intentions, was seized and clapped up in the Gatehouse.

Mr. Goodwynne Wharton* was taken into custody by one of the messengers, and examined touching a complaint sent against him from one of his Majesty's garrisons (as if he did somewhat he ought not about his Majesty's fortifications), but is again released upon bail, before one of the judges.

* Goodwin Wharton was the second son of Philip fourth Lord Wharton and Jane his second wife, daughter and heiress of Arthur Goodwin, Esq. of Upper Winchendon, Bucks. He was consequently brother of Thomas Marquis of Wharton.

We mentioned in our last the choosing Sir John Chapman Lord Mayor, and Sir Humphry Edwynne and Mr. Fleett Sheriffs, for this next year, and Sir Peter Rich to be Chamberlain; but we do not hear yet who is to be Recorder; Sir George Treby being said to have refused it. Mr. Common Serjeant acted at the Old Bayly this sessions for want of a Recorder.

The Bishops are said to have received command from his Majesty to deliver him in writing what they at several times spoke, which some think may be printed. The Archbishop of Canterbury has also prepared a form of prayers to be used upon occasion of the danger that threatens the kingdom at present, which is in the press.*

* It would appear by an article in the Diary of Henry Lord Clarendon, that it was the opinion of the day, that the King was deceiving the Bishops, or, to use a plainer term, making fools of them. "October 12th. I waited on the Princess (of Denmark.) She told me she wished the Bishops were out of town; 'for,' said she, 'it is plain they can do no good. The King will not hearken to them, and they will but expose themselves by being here.' I told her they were all going to their dioceses."

The wind has continued westerly for these ten days past, which we believe obstructs the coming of any letters from Holland, and keeps back the Dutch fleet. Nor do we yet know what certainty there is in the report as if the Dutch had declared war against France.

Some of the squadron of ships that cruised in the Mediterranean are returned, and joined to his Majesty's fleet now in the mouth of the river.

There are not above a thousand men yet landed at Chester out of Ireland, notwithstanding the great noise of our jealous spirits about the City of London, as if there were a thousand for each hundred. We have no foreign mail come in as yet, three being wanting from Holland, three from France, and four from Flanders.

For John Ellis, Esq. Secretary to the
    Commissioners of the Revenue in
    Ireland.

CCV.

The Prince of Orange's Speech to the States.

Hague, Oct. 13th, Old Stile.

MY LORDS,*

I AM going to the navy to embark. I hope you do not take it ill that I do not make it known to you all where I am going. I will assure your Lordships, that what I am designing is for the good of the Protestant religion in general, and of your State in particular, as is not unknown to some among you. I will either succeed in it, or spend my blood to the last drop. My Lords, your trust in me, and kindness to me at this time, is unbounded. If I live, and make it not the business of my life to make your Lordships suitable returns

---

* This speech and the answer to it have been often published before ; but as in the MS. they are numbered and bound up with the letters, and as they connect themselves with the details contained in many of these, I have thought it better to give them in their proper place.

for it, may God blast all my designs, and let me pass for the most ungrateful wretch that ever lived !

Heer Fagell's answer, by order.

SIR,

My Lords the States are not at all displeased that you conceal from them your design. They do repose an entire confidence in your Highness's conduct, zeal to the Protestant religion, and affection to their State; otherwise they would never have given you the absolute disposal of their navy, their armies, and their money. My Lord, the States wish you all success in your designs, and have ordered a public fast and prayers to God, for your success, through all their dominions; and beg it of your Highness not to venture your life and person unnecessarily ; for though their navy and their army be the very sinews of their State, your person is more considerable to them than both.

CCVI.

Full Drawing-room.—Reports respecting the Dutch.—Prince
of Wales christened.—Foreign news.

London, Oct. 16th, 1688.

NEVER place was more thronged than
our drawing-room at Whitehall this evening.
The Dutch have ebbed and flowed these three
days in the report of the vulgar : one hour a
lying postmaster, from Newport, put a story
five years old upon us, that twelve of their best
men of war were stranded, and the men lost ;
which, by the wonderful joy appeared in every
Catholic face, showed how much fear was in
their hearts : the truth, I am confident, is, that
their fleet is much shattered, but possibly repaired by this time, and the upland-men much
disordered by sea-weather.   Zitters says, to-
morrow he will tell the King they never designed coming hither ; but I am not of his mind,
and imagine we shall find it by next Sunday or

Monday.   Some vessels this morning appeared off the Gun-fleet, but I doubt not but they were some of our tenders.   Our fleet are sailed from the buoy of the Ard-sand last night.   The wind is east-north-east, and thereabouts, all day.

The Prince of Wales was christened yesterday,* and called James Francis Edward ; Pope's Nuncio† and Queen Dowager gossips ; the Catholic Court was fine, and the show great.   The French are like to come off very ill from Philipsburgh ; for they lose great numbers, are up to the middle in the trenches, and cruelly infested with water.   The Pope is so angry with the French King, and consequently his faction, that Cardinal d'Estrées‡ and another

---

* " In the midst of all these distractions, the King caused the Prince of Wales to be solemnly baptized ; the Pope, represented by his Nuncio, being Godfather, and the Queen Dowager Godmother.   Father Saban officiated, and named him James Francis Edward."—Rapin.

† The Cardinal Ferdinand Dada, Archbishop of Amasia.

‡ Cæsar Cardinal d'Estrées, son of the first Marshal d'Estrées.   He was much employed by Lewis the Fourteenth in his various negotiations with the Princes of Italy.

fellow with a hard name, are commanded out of Rome and his territories.

For John Ellis, Esq. Secretary of His
Majesty's Revenue in Dublin.
Ireland. Dublin.

CCVII.

16th Oct. 1688.

THE wind hath been fair these three days, and we expect the Dutch Armada will appear every minute upon the coast.

O. WYNNE.

CCVIII.

Irish troops disorderly.—Dutch fleet shattered.—The King calls the Judges, &c. together.—Ill treatment of the writer.

London, Oct. 23d, 1688.

OUR Irish tall fellows* came into Holbourne, where they quarter, on Saturday; on

* A portion of the Irish army, which had been sent for over by James to assist in defending him in his present emergency. See Letter 203.

Sunday a squabble with the neighbourhood, but not much hurt, though the world talk of murder, ravishment, &c. There seems to be little use for them at last; for our last accounts from Holland say a mighty sickness amongst men and horses, and the Prince of Orange very melancholy. They were much shattered, to be sure, and concealed their harm what they could. We begin to vapour here apace, and strive for troops. I wish myself quit of some burthensome horses; for I look upon the terror over, but what they will have by our fleet and fireships, if the wind would shrink but to a moderate gale. Yesterday, before the preceding tidings came, was held a high Council here. There were summoned the Lords Spiritual and Temporal here or hereabouts, the Judges, (whereof Sir Tho. Stringer, to-day a new one, in the place of Allibone, dead,) Lord Mayor of London, Aldermen and Sheriffs, and the eminent lawyers; where the King, in short, told them, that he did not doubt but they were all satisfied the design of Holland was to invade him; that he was firmly resolved to oppose them in person; and because he knew not how Providence might dispose of him, he had called them there, he hoped, to convince them of the barbarity of the report that had painted him so unnatural that he would debar his own daughters from the right of succeeding him, to give his kingdoms to a supposititious son; therefore, he offered the proof to be scanned before them of the legality of his son the Prince's birth, which was the Queen Dowager's oath, Lady Roscommon,* Lady Bellasis,† Arran, and

* Frances (Boyle) eldest daughter of Richard first Earl of Burlington, and of his wife Elizabeth Clifford, daughter and heiress of Henry Earl of Cumberland. This lady was first the wife of Colonel Courtenay, and after his death married, in 1682, the celebrated Wentworth (Dillon) fourth Earl of Roscommon, whom she survived many years.

† Susan, daughter and coheiress of Sir William Airemine, of Osgodby, Bart. She married Sir Henry Bellasyse, K.B. eldest son of John Lord Bellasyse, who was killed during his father's lifetime. She is said to have intrigued with Charles the Second, who created her in consequence, in 1674, Baroness Bellasyse of Osgodby for life. She subsequently married ―― Fortrey, of Chequers, Esq. whom she survived. She died March 6th, 1713.

Sunderland, and many others, that swore very plainly and positively in the matter; and his Majesty at last declared, upon his honour, that he had often laid his hand upon the Queen's belly, and felt the child stir. This will be registered in Chancery after the same manner the late King's Declaration was of the Duke of Monmouth's illegitimacy. We are low in the pocket at Court, and so am I that lie now in the nearer neighbourhood of it; therefore, hereafter direct your's to me at Mr. Mic^{ll}. East's in Ax-yard, King-street, Westminster. Sarsefeild said he had not answered my note at Dublin, but would do it here, which I faintly hope. If you can do any good with Mr. Eustace, send me a bill.

I have been scandalized and used like a dog by Lords Dartmouth and Preston : they casting out in their cups that I was a spy employed by the Priests to give intelligence and drive that interest. God knows how far I have been from such designs, or injuring any body from the freedom of their private discourse ; yet is this whispered about to my great trouble; and upon taxing Lord Preston, he denies all with imprecations; and Mr. Musgrave pretends to answer for my Lord Dartmouth, that he never either said or thought such a thing. I could well enough sit down with this dirt thrown at me, knowing it will rub off when it is dry, but that the thought, I fear, sticks with my Lord D. of Ormonde. You have known some of my nearest thoughts: if you think I deserve your good word, say something to him in your next.

     Mr. Ellis.

For John Ellis, Esq. Secretary of his
    Majesty's Revenue in Ireland,
Ireland.   At Dublin.

CCIX.

23d Oct. 1688.

MR. ELLIS,

I HAVE had two letters lately from you, the later of which was given me yesterday by Markham, who owns your care of him in the time of his sickness; and I do allow of the expenses you were at on his behalf during that time, and for his coming hither, though they exceeded what I thought fit to give him for his maintenance till he should be otherwise provided for. I thank you for the advertisements you have given me relating to my regiment, and desire to hear from you as matter shall offer.

ORMONDE.

To John Ellis, Esq. at the Custom-
house in   Dublin.

CCX.

No certain news.—Rumours from Philipsburgh, Constantinople, and Holland.—Colonel Sydney's books searched, &c.

London, Oct. 27th, 1688.

SIR,

OUR mails from abroad have for this
fortnight hung out, and we may reasonably
conclude them to be stopped, as well by the
wind as otherwise; so that our advices from
abroad are very scanty, and we know not well
how matters go at Philipsburgh : wagers are
laid it will not be taken this bout. It is certain
the Dauphin has hard labour, though his glory
will be the greater if he succeeds. But at the
coming away of our last Brussels letters, a report just began to spring up in that town, that
the Dauphin had broke up the siege, and con-
verted it into a blockade ; but as we know not
to whom or whence this advice came thither,
we must suspend affording it absolute credit.

Our letters from Constantinople, of August
24th, assure you that they have not been in

any trouble or disturbance since the rebellion of the Zorbas, which was just after the election of the new Emperor; and that especially the English live in perfect peace, and have more civility shown them, and enjoying more privileges, than formerly; that the Grand Vizier is now raising men to go in person towards Belgrade; that there are sixteen sail of Venetian men-of-war lying at the mouth of the Dardanelles, though without performing much, only keeping out small vessels from Alexandria, which renders things very dear at Constantinople.

The wind did again come about yesterday to the south-east, which was fair to the Dutch; so that it is probable they took hold of the opportunity to come away, especially the nights being so clear and light; but to-day is south-west again.

Some tell us of the Prince of Orange's being sick, and that the bloody flux reigns in their fleet. Some foot and horse having been embarked these three weeks or a month, and most of them people that have never seen the sea before, they are supposed to be in a sweet condition.

The first tempest disabled several of their best ships, three weeks ago; but the storm of last Saturday night was yet more violent, so that we expect with impatience to know how the Dutch fleet escaped it, thirty of their men-of-war having been seen abroad that day under sail, some few hours before the storm began, which in all likelihood forced them back again.

The Count of Nassau, General of the Horse, and the Count of Solms, are said to be on board the Hollands fleet; and they tell us, that during the Prince of Orange's absence, the Count of Flodrop, the Prince Waldeck, and Lieutenant-general Alva, will have the command on the frontiers of Gelderland; Lieutenant-general Delvich, upon those of Overyssell; the Count of Horn and Lieutenant-general Webnom, in Flanders; and Major-General Obdam, at Boisleduc.

The King's fleet, under my Lord Dartmouth, were seen off of Essex sailing towards the Gun-fleet; they were thirty-three men-of-war in number, and sixteen fire-ships. Some of the biggest ships are yet in the River, and will follow very speedily.

The City of London chose one Mr. R. Sumners to be their Recorder, but he declined it; and since they have elected Mr. Selby.

Mr. Serjeant Stringer* (whose son married the Lord Chancellor's daughter) is made Puisne Judge of the King's Bench, in the room of Judge Allybone, lately deceased.

Great noise has been made about a large sum of money and arms found in a milliner's house in the Pell Mell, but we are very well informed it is only a mistake; and that though there were several trunks searched, yet there was nothing in them but books, which they say belong to Colonel Sidney, who went into Holland some while since.

* Sir Thomas Stringer, Knight, of Darrance, near Enfield, in Middlesex. His son, William Stringer, Esq. had married Margaret Jefferies, the Chancellor's eldest daughter.

The depositions about the birth of the Prince of Wales are to be enrolled in Chancery, and several lords and ladies attended this day to that purpose.

Our Cologne letters inform us that 600 men more of the troops of the Circle were entered that town to reinforce its garrison, and there was going to be a camp of 25 or 30,000 men near Wesell, and a magazine established at Duisburg* for their subsistence, in case of marching ; that there will be 8000 of the Hollands troops, and that the rest will be furnished by the Circles of Westphalia and Lower Saxony. Coblentz is not invested.

For John Ellis, Esq. Secretary to the
   Commissioners for the Revenue of
   Ireland,   At Dublin.

---

* A strong town in the Duchy of Cleves, situated on the right bank of the Rhine.

CCXI.

27th Oct. 1688.

We have neither letters nor Gazettes from Holland, and the Marquis* is forced to keep house and to live in ignorance, and to keep us so too. The Prince of Orange was in last Saturday's storm : he embarked the 19th ; and last Sunday he was driven back, in a shattered condition, upon the Dutch coast. We know not the particulars of his loss : three or four hundred horse are said to be thrown overboard, and all the rest in disorder : others say seventy or eighty, and some small craft lost and sunk, and two men-of-war disabled. My Lord Preston is made Secretary of State, and my Lord of Middleton removes to my Lord of Sunderland's office. Perhaps I may stick with one of

* Probably Lord Halifax.

hem still; but wherever I am, I shall always be
most faithfully,

Yours.

I had four packets from you on Thursday.

For John Ellis, Esq. Secretary for the
Revenue of Ireland,
At Dublin.

CCXII.

Lord Sunderland's disgrace, and reasons assigned for it.—
Rumours of other changes.—Foreign news.—Catholic Chapel in London destroyed.

London, Oct. 30th, 1688.

DEAR SIR,

I DOUBT not but the letters on Saturday would tell you what accident had happened to Lord Sunderland, and that Lord Preston
had the Seals. It was a great surprise to the
first, by what we can judge, and what he vows
now, that not two hours before my Lord Mid-

dleton came to demand the Seals of him from the King, he parted from him never more or better established in his favour. The secret Treaty with France, or something like it, has been his overthrow. He retires to Windsor at present, till affairs are so settled that he may move where he best likes : his Presidentship is not disposed of. We think there are more great men shook : some think the Chancellor and Godolphin ; others, Herbert and Butler.* The first I look upon as surely one ; and if Nottingham will sit with Papists, he succeeds ; otherwise, Herbert and Butler. I think, the other. The Gazette is indifferent just in the account yesterday, that letters of the 23d said a battalion of Foot was sent for from Mastreich, and the Boors were to furnish a thousand horse to recruit the diseased and dead by the late storms. The wind is now fair, and hath been so twenty-four hours ; so that we are like

* Chief Justice Herbert and Sir Nicholas Butler.

to have them, if our naval force of thirty-five, ying now in the Gun-fleet, stop them not. The French cannot yet get Philipsburgh, but have a great body of men marching into the territories of Liege. Our London boys, last night, after the mirth of the Lord Mayor's show, demolished the Mass-house in Lyme-street, and burned all the altar implements. The dominion of the Tower will be left in old Werden's hands, I think ; and a detachment of English entire in it, from all the regiments. Vic. Barrinton is in town. You may say safely what you please to your old friend.

For John Ellis, Esq. Secretary of His
   Majesty's Revenue in Ireland,
Ireland.   Dublin.

CCXIII.

Loss of the Dutch in the Storm.

30th Oct. 1688.

SIR,

WE are now come a little nearer to you and the South,* being removed from one office to the other by the change made by the dismission of the Earl of Sunderland, though I cannot hope I may be any thing more useful to you here than I was in the other province. Couriers and letters agree that the Dutch lost above a thousand horse in the late storm. The King said this day twelve hundred, a man-of-war or two disabled, and some of their transportation

* The two Secretaries of State at this time divided the affairs of Europe between them, and were called,—the one, the Secretary of State for the Northern Department or Province; and the other, the Secretary of State for the Southern Department. The affairs of Ireland belonged to the Southern Department; to which circumstance the expression in the text alludes.

boats dispersed, if not sunk.* Yet the wind is full fair for them, and we expect to hear of them every moment ; but hope my Lord Dartmouth may speak with them by the way.

I am, Sir,

Your most obedient servant,

O. WYNNE.

The embargo is off, and we begin to have letters again.

For the much honoured John
Ellis, Esq. Secretary for the
Revenue of Ireland,
At Dublin.

* Burnet, who was on board the Dutch fleet, gives the following account of this disaster:—" At last, on the nineteenth of October, the Prince went aboard, and the whole fleet sailed out that night. But the next day the wind turned into the north, and settled in the north-west. At night a great storm rose. We wrought against it all that night, and the next day ; but it was in vain to struggle any longer. And so vast a fleet run no small hazard, being obliged to keep together, and yet not to come too near one another. On the twenty-first in the afternoon the signal was given to go in again ; and on the twenty-second, the far greater part got safe into port. Many ships were at first wanting, and were believed to be lost ;

CCXIV.

Proofs of the Prince of Wales's Birth sent to the Princess of Denmark.—King orders a proclamation.—Bishops with the King.—Rumours and fears respecting the Dutch.— Foreign news.

London, Nov. 3d, 1688.

His Majesty hath ordered in Council that the whole Privy Council should wait on her Highness the Princess of Denmark, with a copy of the Depositions which were taken and sworn unto in Council, touching the birth of the Prince of Wales.

His Majesty having notice that a printed paper, called the Prince of Orange's Declaration, is dispersed about the town, and the disperser himself (who is now in Newgate) was seized, (as we told you in our last,) with seve-

but after a few days all came in. There was not one ship lost; nor so much as any one man, except one that was blown from the shrouds into the sea. Some ships were so shattered, that as soon as they came in and all was taken out of them, they immediately sunk down. Only five hundred horses died for want of air."

ral about him : It is ordered that a proclamation be published forthwith, forbidding all persons, upon pain of high treason, to read, write,
disperse, or conceal any of the said Declarations, but give notice thereof to the next Justice of Peace.

Yesterday the Archbishop and all the Bishops about town were summoned to attend the
King. What passed is not certainly known ;
but most people do conclude it was the King's
pleasure to communicate to them that part of the
Prince of Orange's Declaration which concerned them and the clergy, it being, as we hear,
pretended in the said Declaration, that the
clergy, among others, had invited the Prince of
Orange to come over. What the said Bishops
will do, time must tell us.

The wind hath been very strong and fair for
the Dutch these five days ; and yet there are
vessels come into this River, which saw their
fleet on the other side on Tuesday and Wednesday last ; and letters from the best hands
in Holland, by way of Flanders, dated from

VOL. II.   T

the Hague on Tuesday last, do affirm they
will not be ready to sail these eight days.   On
the other hand, a master of a ship, of great
credit on the Exchange, that set sail on Wednesday night from the Maze, affirms that the
Dutch set sail that evening before him ; and
this his assertion is confirmed by letters from
Nieuport,* dated on Thursday last.

In meanwhile several people, come from the
country, report to have heard the noise of guns
going off.   Whence some fancy that the fleets
may have been engaged ; but having no account from any good hands, there is no credit
to be given it ; and it is more probable that it
was some more ships sailing out of the River
to go and join the fleet, which rides about
the Galloper.

The letters I mentioned from Nieuport of
the 11th of September, new style, tell us the
Emperor and Empire have declared war against
France, confess Philipsburgh being taken, and

* A town with a harbour on the coast of Flanders,
situated about eleven miles south-west of Ostend.

the Dolphin's march towards Manheim, though that at that very moment guineas are very plentifully offered in town, not only of Philipsburgh's holding out still, but of its relief; insomuch that we would swear there was a conspiracy against the Dolphin's glory. At the same time, the Flemming advices would pretend still to assure us the most Christian King hath sent three expresses to Constantinople to assure the Porte of his having attacked the Emperor and the Empire, with assurance that he will give them their handfulls; and therefore advises the Grand Seignior not to listen to any proposals of peace, but to use his utmost efforts upon the side of Belgrade, smoothing of him with hopes of great advantages; but those advertisements come through such partial hands, the Spaniard adherents, that they will merit better confirmation. The same advices tell us of the Elector of Saxony's march towards the Rhine, with a body of at least 30,000 men; and another body of Hollanders, Brandenburghers, and others, much about the same number, are approaching Cologne, to make head against the enterprises of the French.

For John Ellis, Esq. Secretary to the
    Commissioners for the Revenue
    of Ireland,   At Dublin.

CCXV.

Declaration of C. Loveseto respecting the Dutch Fleet.

Nov. 3d, 1688.

MR. Charles Loveseto, Master of the Loyal Joseph, of London, saith, that he came from the Brill, in Holland, on Wednesday last in the evening, being the 31st of October 1688 ; and that about four o'clock, the same afternoon, he saw the Dutch fleet, which is reported to be about five hundred sail of great and small ships, under sail ; and, as near as he could guess, they steered their course to sea-ward, but cannot tell what course they went : that it is reported that there are several English gentlemen amongst them; and that the Lord Mordaunt, Lord Wiltshire,* Lord Macclesfield, and Admiral Herbert, are there.

CHARLES LOVESETO.

---

* Charles (Powlett) Earl of Wiltshire, eldest son of the Marquis of Winchester. He had been for some time with the Prince of Orange. In 1699, he succeeded his father, who had been created Duke of Bolton. He was Lord Lieutenant of the counties of Dorset, Southampton, Carmarthen, and Glamorgan. In 1714, he was made a Knight of the Garter; in 1715, he was Lord Chamberlain; in 1717, Lord Lieutenant of Ireland; and died January 21st, 1722. The father of Lord Wiltshire, Charles sixth Marquis of Winchester and first Duke of Bolton, who contributed considerably to the success of the Revolution, was one of the most eccentric of men. Reresby gives the following curious account of him:—
" In the midst of the impending dangers which seemed to threaten us (1687), there was a nobleman, the Marquis of Winchester, who had by his conduct persuaded some people to think him mad, though he certainly acted upon principles of great human prudence. This gentleman passing through Yorkshire, in his way to London, I went to pay him a visit. He had four coaches and an hundred horses in his retinue, and stayed ten days at a house he borrowed in our parts. His custom was to dine at six or seven in the evening, and his meal always lasted till six or seven the next morning; during which he sometimes drank, sometimes he listened to

CCXVI.

6th Nov. 1688.

SIR,

JUST now, at seven, we hear the Dutch fleet (500 sail) was put into Torbay, Exmouth,

music, sometimes he fell into discourse, sometimes he took tobacco, and sometimes he ate his victuals, while the company had free choice to sit or rise, to go or come, to sleep or not.   The dishes and bottles were all the time before them on the table.   And when it was morning, he would hunt or hawk, if the weather was fair ; if not, he would dance, go to bed at eleven, and repose himself till the evening.   Notwithstanding this great irregularity, he was a man of great sense ; and though, as I just now said, some took him to be mad, it is certain his meaning was to keep himself out of the way of more serious censure in these ticklish days, and preserve his estate, which he took great care of."   Burnet's character of him is less favourable : " This year (1699) died the Marquis of Winchester, whom the King had created Duke of Bolton.   He was a man of a strange mixture : he had the spleen to a high degree, and affected an extravagant behaviour.   For many weeks he would take a conceit not to speak one word ; and at other times, he would not open his mouth till such an hour of the day, when he thought the air was pure.   He changed the day into night, and often hunted by torch-light ; and took all sorts of liberties to himself, many of and Dartmouth: all conclude they design to Bristoll, but will take Exeter and other places in the way. We here are in good heart, though in some hurry, and hope for good success. Our enemies having fed these two months upon a biscuit, two herrings, and a pint of Dortz Engelze a-day, we hope to find their noble courage much cast down. When any thing occurs, and that I have a minute's time, I shall give you part of it. A Counter-Declaration is sent to the press.

Mr. Ellis.

For John Ellis, Esq. Secretary for the
Revenue of Ireland,   At Dublin.

---

which were very disagreeable to those about him. In the end of King Charles's time, and during King James's reign, he affected an appearance of folly, which afterwards he compared to Junius Brutus's behaviour under the Tarquins. With all this, he was a very knowing and a very crafty politic man; and was an artful flatterer, when that was necessary to compass his end, in which generally he was successful. He was a man of a profuse expense, and of a most ravenous avarice to support that: and though he was much hated, yet he carried matters before him with such authority and success, that he was in all respects the great riddle of the age."

CCXVII.

The Dutch landed.—Troops marching westward, &c.

London, 6th Nov. 1688, nine at night, at the
Ship Tavern with several of your friends.

SIR,

SUNDAY and yesterday the King * had
an account of the Dutch fleet, consisting of
above 400 sail, passed the Downs, Dover, and
Isle of Weight, having slipped by the King's
fleet, that then lay at the Galloper off of Harwich in expectation that the Dutch intended
for the north, but they stood up the Channel
to the westward : and just now is come in an
express, that gives an account that they are
landed, the Prince of Orange with them, &c. at
Torr-Bay, Exmouth, and Dartmouth, and no
doubt will be masters of Exon by the next

* While William was invading his kingdom, James appears to have been occupied in duties of another kind.
Evelyn, in the entry in his Diary of the 6th of November,
1688, mentions, " I saw his Majesty touch for the evil, Piten
the Jesuit, and Warner assisting."

account that can reach this place. My Lord Dartmouth, it is said, passed the Downs Sunday last, in pursuit of them ; but it is believed he was so far behind them, that he can come in for nothing but dry blows, since, for certain, they landed yesterday at twelve o'clock noon. All our land forces are, with all imaginable diligence, marching westward ; and it is believed the King will march to-morrow, but this is only conjecture. Pardon haste and good company, and the present opportunity we have of drinking your health.

I am sincerely yours,
WILL. CULLIFORD.

My service to Mr. Dickinson : pray show him this, for I have not time to write to him ; nor to say more, but service to him and all friends. Vale.

For John Ellis, Esq. Secretary to the
   Honourable the Commissioners of
   His Majesty's Revenue of Ireland,
   at the Custom House,
              In Dublin.

CCXVIII.

Prince of Orange in Torbay.—Lord Bath about to quit Exeter.—Rumours from Scotland.—Bishops with the King.

London, Nov. 6th, 1688.

Now our expectations are at a full point; for, yesterday, the small craft that belonged to the Prince of Orange's fleet set into Torbay, and fell to land at Dartmouth and Exmouth;* and

* Burnet's account of the voyage is as follows.—" On the first of November, O. S. we sailed out with the evening tide ; but made little way that night, that so our fleet might come out, and move in order. We tried next day till noon, if it was possible to sail northward; but the wind was so strong, and full in the east, that we could not move that way. About noon the signal was given to steer westward. This wind not only diverted us from that unhappy course, but it kept the English fleet in the river ; so that it was not possible for them to come out, though they were come down as far as the Gun-fleet. By this means, we had the sea open to us, with a fair wind and a safe navigation. On the third we past between Dover and Calais, and before night came in sight of the Isle of Wight. The next day being the day in which the Prince was both born and married, he fancied, if he could land that day, it would look auspicious to the army, and animate the soldiers. But we all, who considered that the day following being Gunpowder Treason day, our landing that day his Highness surely dined in Exeter to-day, for my Lord of Bath* that was there, writes he should in few hours be forced to quit the town, so he would retire to his garrison at Plymouth, where was Earl of Huntingdon's regiment only, and defend that as long as he could. We shall march now in few days, and have the prospect

might have a good effect on the minds of the English nation, were better pleased to see that we could land no sooner. Torbay was thought the best place for our great fleet to lie in ; and it was resolved to land the army where it could be best done near it."

* John (Granville) first Earl of Bath. He had been in great favour with Charles the Second, and was permitted by him to remain in the room when the King on his death-bed received the Sacrament from Huddleston, the Popish priest. He appears, from Burnet, to have been doubtful which side he should take upon the present occasion, or rather to have been inclined to wait till he saw which side was strongest. " The Earl of Bath, who was Governor of Plymouth, had sent, by Russell, a promise to the Prince to come and join him. Yet it was not likely, that he would be so forward to receive us at our first coming. The delays he made afterwards, pretending that he was managing the garrison, whereas he was still staying till he saw how the matter was likely to be decided, showed us how fatal it had proved, if we had been forced to sail on to Plymouth."—Burnet, History of his Own Times.

of a miserable winter's war. We have no account of our fleet, which was sent after them. The Dutch men of war lay in a line to guard the boats that were landing the men. I wish you peace in your kingdom and health: the former is now gone in this, and the fatigue of a winter's campaign is but an ill prospect for the other. Some think Macky,* with a good body, as Lord Lorne,† &c. are got to Scotland, to see what hands are to be made there.

---

* " Mackay, a general officer, that had long served in Holland with great reputation, and who was the finest man I ever knew, in a military way, was sent down to command the army in Scotland. He was one of the best officers of the age, when he had nothing to do but to obey and execute orders: for he was both diligent, obliging, and brave; but he was not so fitted to command."——Burnet's Account of the year 1689. He commanded at the battle of Killicrankie against Lord Dundee. He afterwards served in Ireland; and was killed at the battle of Steenkirk, in 1692.

† This was Archibald (Campbell) tenth Earl of Argyll; eldest son of the ninth Earl, who was beheaded in 1685. He had been in Holland, and came over with William. In 1701, he was created Duke of Argyll. William the Third was accustomed to say of him, that " he got more truth from Ar-

The Bishops, viz. Canterbury, Rochester, Peterborough, London,* were with the King this morning. Something very bold was said, for neither party was pleased, by their countenances at parting. Our friend B. Jon. I fear in his country now, &c.

For John Ellis, Esq. Secretary of His
   Majesty's Revenue in Ireland,
Ireland.   Dublin.

---

gyll, than from all the rest of his servants in Scotland, because he had the courage to speak out what others did not even venture to hint."

* Sancroft, Sprat, White, and Compton. The King wanted them to make a Declaration, expressing their dislike of the Prince of Orange's coming. This they refused to do, unless the Temporal Peers would join them in it. Lord Clarendon mentions the interview of the Bishops with James on the 6th of November, in the following words, which agree exactly with what is said in this letter :—" The Bishops were with the King to-day ; but his Majesty was not pleased with what they said to him."

CCXIX.

Private business.—Prince of Orange.—King's forces moving
to Salisbury.—Changes in the Secretary of State's offices.

Whitehall, 10th Nov. 1688.

SIR,

My last to you bore date the 13th of
October, in answer to your's of the 5th, and
told you that I had received the twenty pounds
from Mr. Bedford. I did then trouble you
with a letter to Mr. James Tisdall, of whom I
desired you to receive a little money for me.

Since that time I have spoke to Mr. Hoare
the goldsmith, who gives you his humble service. I had no occasion to speak to him of
the money, that is, whether it were ready for
you at your call, because I have no directions
so to do, neither would I give him cause to
suspect that I mistrusted. I hear nothing amiss
yet of him or the other goldsmith, nor had I
occasion to receive any money since from a
goldsmith, whereby to try their temper; so

hat I cannot say if you were here and desired your money, you would not be paid by them.

I make no doubt but that you have had an account of the Prince of Orange's beginning to land his forces, near Dartmouth, on the 5th instant. The King's forces are drawing that way; and, I think, may meet together somewhere about Salisbury Plains, about the end of the next week.

Sir Robert Southwell says that he lately sent you the copy of what Mr. Mulys answers to your queries; and by a letter from him I find, that he much desires something from you on that subject, according to his letter.

You cannot but hear of the alterations in the Secretaries' offices. Mr. Bridgman and Dr. Wynn are in my Lord Middleton's office; Mr. Warre and Mr. Fergus Grahme are in my Lord Preston's, and Mr. Tempest attends my Lord Preston's private affairs in the office. I am, with all respect, Sir,

Your most humble servant,
PHIL. MADOX.

About two o'clock, this afternoon, his Majesty's train of artillery passed through Piccadilly.

For John Ellis, Esq. Secretary of His
Majesty's Revenue in Ireland,
At Dublin.

CCXX.

Prince of Orange at Exeter.—The country not eager to join him.

10th Nov. 1688.

SIR,

YOUR'S of the 24th past are but just come in. The Prince of Orange is at Exeter since yesterday 20 ᵐ. strong : he hath bespoke 10 ᵐ. pairs of shoes. The country is not fond of him, nor forward to run in to him. They keep good order, but cannot prevail with Colonel Strangways,* or any of his neighbours, to come at them ; but they send their inviting

---

* Strangeways of Melbury in Dorsetshire, a gentleman of good family, and ancestor by females of Lord Ilchester.

letters unopened up to the King. They want oxen and horses for draft. Our artillery went out this day; the King follows next Thursday; so that you will imagine we are here in hurry and some confusion. We seized a bag of letters and a boat of theirs going for Holland.

Mr. Ellis, Mr. Melvill, &c.

For John Ellis, Esq. Secretary
for the Revenue of Ireland,
At Dublin.

CCXXI.

Details respecting the Prince of Orange and his Army at Exeter.—The Bishop and Chapter run away on his coming. —Mails stopped.—London lads unruly.—Duke of Beaufort's arm broken.

London, Nov. 13th, 1688.

SIR,

IT is said the Prince of Orange is now settled at Exeter as his head-quarters; but that most of his companions are lodged in the neighbouring towns ten or fifteen miles off. The 6000 pair of shoes which he bespoke at Exeter are not yet ready, and so we know not what way they intend to take. Others think that the bespeaking these shoes was but a trick to drill on time, till they could see if any part of England would come in to them. But we are assured their allies come on but slowly, all the West being quiet, and almost unconcerned at their being there, while they pay for what they have. Some of the scurf and meaner part run in to them as they would to see a show, but generally retreat the next day ; most of our Western people having, ever since Monmouth's time, been much troubled with dreams of gibbets, &c.

The Dean and Chapter, as well as the Bishop,* ran away at their coming into Exeter ; and so would most of the inhabitants, but that it happens to be a.great fair-time there.

They stop and rifle all mails and letters that

* Thomas Lamplugh, who was also Dean of Rochester. He was shortly after this translated to the see of York.

pass that way; and the doing of it now in fair-time does, in some people's opinion, seem as if they looked for money, and bills of exchange, and not letters of news. Some tell us, they begin to plunder and imprison, notwithstanding they have promised the contrary, having taken violently 300*l.* from the Collector of Excise, and thrown him into prison.

Though there has been a great noise, as if some men of quality, Mr. Wharton* and others, were gone in to the invaders; yet it proves false, for Mr. Wharton was seen since at Court, and other places where he frequents.

Some few of the maltsters and butchers of Buckinghamshire (most commonly those that owe more than they can pay) are missing, and supposed to be run away in hopes to plunder, not to pay their creditors.

Great endeavours are used to prevail with the lads of London to be troublesome, under the pretence of pulling down the Popish chapels

* The Honourable Goodwin Wharton, mentioned before, in Letter 204.

in Lime-street, Bucklersbury, and St. John's.
Some scores of them have rendezvoused these
two last nights; but upon beat of drum, and
appearing of any small part of the militia, have
scampered away, and by flight provided for
their safety: the Lord Mayor and Lieutenancy of the City, as well as the officers of the
county of Middlesex, keeping a strict eye to
the least motion that is made by these young
mutineers.

Our fleet is still about the Downs, and that
of the Dutch about Torbay; several of their
sea and land men desert them. Last night a
lieutenant of one of their men-of-war was
examined at the Council in Whitehall: he was
originally a Scotsman, and says their fleet is
but forty-four sail, and twelve fire-ships, and
no great vessels among them, and that they
begin to want provisions.

We have no farther apprehension of a party
of their fleet being gone northward; for that
Major-General Mackay, who was to command

1em, was one of the first who landed in the
Vest.

We are told the Duke of Beaufort has broke
is arm at Bristol; which, if true, is the greater
aischance at this time that his presence is so
ecessary for the King's service in that place.

The French go on with their conquest in
Germany without control, it being sleeping-
me with the Germans, who did not expect a
ampaign in the depth of winter. All the Pa-
tinate is surrendered, and many of the locks
f the Rhine in the Electorate of Cologne,
Iayence, and Treves. Coblentz, the famous
aagazine and fountain of good Rhenish wine,
 bombarded, and quite ruined to the ground;*
ut the French of a sudden retired from be-
ore it, likely to go upon some design that
equired more haste. The French are draw-

* " On bombarde Coblentz pour punir l'Electeur de Trèves
y avoir reçu des troupes de l'Electeur de Saxe ; on s'empare
assi de Trèves, Spire, et Worms."—President Henault,
brégé Chronologique.

ing men together towards the borders of Holland, being loth to slip the opportunity of the Prince of Orange's absence with the chief and best of the Dutch officers.

For John Ellis, Esq. Secretary to the
    Commissioners for the Revenue of
    Ireland,   At Dublin.

CCXXII.

Lord Lovelace and his followers taken at Cirencester.—Burnet in the Cathedral at Exeter.—Details respecting the Prince of Orange.

London, Nov. 15th, 1688.
SIR,

LAST night came an express from Cirencester in Gloucestershire, with an account that the Lord Lovelace * riding through that

* John third Lord Lovelace was an early and strenuous friend of the Revolution. In Lysons' Magna Britannia, in the account of Hurley in Berkshire, is the following passage :—" Lady Place, the seat of Mr. Kempenfelt, was built about the year 1600, by Sir Richard Lovelace. It was fitted

town with a strong party of about one hundred horse very well armed, was stopped by the militia of the county ; and they requiring of him what was his business to go so armed, and whither he was a-going ; but his Lordship not giving any good answer of himself or his company, thought it his best way to fight his passage through ; and charging the militia, which was but part of a troop, they came to blows ; and in the scuffle, one Major Lowridge and his son, who commanded the militia, were killed ; one Captain Williams and five or six more, wounded ; but we do not yet hear how many of the rebels were killed, only that the Lord

up with great splendour by John Lord Lovelace, in the reign of King William. The hall and staircase are very magnificent, &c. Under the hall is a vault, in which, according to tradition, secret meetings were held for promoting the Revolution in 1688 ; and it is farther said, that King William, visiting Lord Lovelace after that period, was taken by his host to see the vault. His present Majesty is also recorded to have visited the same in 1785." The splendour of Lord Lovelace ruined his fortune ; and the greater part of his estate was eventually sold under a decree of the Court of Chancery, for the payment of his debts.

Lovelace and thirteen of his followers were taken, and are now in the gaol at Cirencester.

This party designed to go join the Prince of Orange in the West, from whence the Lord Lovelace had been come but few days; and those with him are supposed to be his tenants and neighbours, but none of any great note that I can yet hear of.

We are told from good hands at Exeter, that Dr. Burnett * has taken possession of the Cathedral, and both preached in it on Sunday last before the Prince of Orange, and then openly read the Prince's Declaration, though the Prince and he well approved of the not reading the King's late Declaration. Burnet sent in the Prince's name to all the clergy, commanding them also to read it, and to read a form of prayer for the Prince's good success;

---

* Gilbert Burnet, afterwards Bishop of Salisbury.—" The Sunday after the Prince's arrival at Exeter, Dr. Burnet mounting the pulpit to read his Declaration, all the canons and part of the congregation left the church, not to be present at the reading."—Rapin.

but they are said to have all unanimously refused and rejected the proposal.

We do not find that any one gentleman of
quality, substance, or estate, is come in to them
from the West; but some from the Eastern
parts of England flock to them, by the means
and interest of those lords and others said to
be already there, as Earl Shrewsbury, Earl
Macclesfield, Lord Mordaunt, one of the
Whartons, Lord Wiltshire, some Scotch Lairds
also.

The Prince has his Privy Council which
meets every day, which consists of the said
lords and other gentlemen, as Major Wildman,* (and some other Oliverians,) together

* " Wildman had been an agitator in Cromwell's army,
and had opposed his Protectorship.   After the Restoration,
he, being looked upon as a high Republican, was kept long in
prison; where he had studied law and physic so much, that
he passed as a man very knowing in those matters.   He had
a way of creating in others a great opinion of his sagacity,
and had great credit with the Duke of Buckingham."—Burnet.   Wildman was a staunch Republican.   He was impli-

with Burnett, Ferguson,* and Balfour,† who is
a Scotch field-preacher, and said to be the man
that murdered the Archbishop of St. Andrew's‡

cated more or less in all the plots of Charles's and James's
reigns.

* " Ferguson was a hot and a bold man, whose spirit was
naturally turned to plotting.   He was always unquiet, and
setting people on to some mischief.   I knew a private thing
of him, by which it appeared he was a profligate knave, and
could cheat those that trusted him entirely.   So, though he,
being a Scottish man, took all the ways he could to be admit-
ted into some acquaintance with me, I would never see him,
or speak with him ; and I did not know his face till the Revolution.   He was cast out by the Presbyterians ; and then
went among the Independents, where his boldness raised him
to some figure, though he was at bottom a very empty man."
—Burnet.—Ferguson had been engaged in Monmouth's Rebellion, after which he fled to Holland, and came over with
the Prince of Orange, as is stated in this letter.

† John Balfour of Burleigh.   He had been, in effect, one
of the most active of the murderers of the Archbishop.

‡ Sharp, Archbishop of St. Andrew's.   He was a cruel,
treacherous, worldly, and time-serving man.   His murder
took place in 1679, and was thus perpetrated :—" When a
party of furious men were riding through a moor near St.
Andrew's, they saw the Archbishop's coach appear.   He was
coming from a council day, and was driving home.   He had
sent some of his servants home before him, to let them know
he was coming, and others he had sent off on compliments ;

about the year 78, and for which he has been
since fled, and protected by the States of Holland.

His Majesty is very well satisfied with the
zeal and care of the militia 'in Gloucestershire,
who behaved themselves so well upon this occasion in taking the Lord Lovelace ; and it is
said his Majesty intends some particular mark
of favour to every one concerned in that action ;
which, as it is much for their own honour and

so that there was no horsemen about the coach. They, seeing
his, concluded, according to their frantic enthusiastic notions,
hat God had now delivered up their greatest enemy into
their hands. Some of them made up to the coach, while the
rest were at scouts riding all about the moor. One of them fired
a pistol at him, which burnt his coat and gown ; but did not
go into his body. Upon this, they perceived he had a magical
secret to secure him against a shot ; and they drew him out
of his coach, and murdered him barbarously, repeating their
strokes till they were sure he was quite dead ; and so they
got clear off, nobody happening to cross the moor all the while.
This was the dismal end of that unhappy man. It struck all
people with horror, and softened his enemies into some ten-
derness ; so that his memory was treated with decency by
those who had very little respect for him during his life."—
Burnet.

for the credit and reputation of the militia of that county, so it is hoped it may prove a good example to the militia of other counties to do their duty likewise.

Some letters frŏm the West say the Prince of Orange intends for Bristol, and thence to Glostershire and to Salop, and that he has abundance of copper and tin boats to use upon the Severn; but of this time must tell us the certainty; and his Majesty has sent some thousands of his army to dispute their passage about Bristol.

Orders are given to stop all passengers, in all parts of England, who have no passes from a Secretary of State; and the militia are to take care in it, as well as the civil magistrate.

For John Ellis, Esq. Secretary to the
  Commissioners for the Revenue of
  Ireland,   At Dublin.

CCXXIII.

King gone to Windsor, and from thence intends to go westward.—Petition for a Free Parliament.

17th Nov. 1688.

JUST now late comes yours of the 3rd. This day at two his Majesty marched for Windsor with the Prince of Wales. They will be to-morrow at Basinstoke or Andover. The Queen is here still! This is melancholy time with us all : what adds to our pain is, that our fleet set sail yesterday, in quest, it is thought, of the Dutch fleet. God send us good success! A petition signed by the Archbishops and several Lords (about seventeen in all) was this noon delivered to his Majesty, praying him to call a free Parliament,* and to prevent the effusion of blood. I know not what answer it had.

Mr. Ellis.

For John Ellis, Esq. Secretary for the
Revenue of Ireland,   At Dublin.

---

* " Nov. 17th. In the morning the Archbishop and the rest of the lords spiritual and temporal who had met, de-

CCXXIV.

The King's Fleet sets sail.—Prince of Orange seizes the King's money.—Bishops with the King.—General News.

London, Nov. 17th, 1688.

SIR,

YESTERDAY his Majesty's fleet, under the Lord Dartmouth, set sail out of the Downs towards the West, the wind N. E. a brisk gale; and it is confidently reported his Lordship's orders are to fight the Dutch.

The Lord Lovelace and his partizans that were taken with him are removed from Cirencester Gaol to Gloster Castle, under a strict guard.

The Prince of Orange continues to seize on the King's money at Exeter. Besides the 300*l.*

livered the Petition to the King, with which his Majesty seemed not pleased, and gave a very short answer to them, to this effect, that he would call a Parliament as soon as it was convenient, but it could not be while the invasion and rebellion lasted."—Diary of Henry Earl of Clarendon ; in which will also be found a long and detailed account of the preparation and presentation of the petition.

we formerly mentioned, we are told now of 4000*l*. more arising from the Customs and Excise.

Yesterday morning, about two o'clock, a fire happened in Leadenhall Market, burning very furiously for a time; but by the care that was taken to extinguish it, no more than two houses were destroyed.

This day was published a Proclamation forbidding the holding of Exeter fair, or any other fair within twenty miles of that place.

Yesterday the Bishops in town attended his Majesty; but how far any persons have expressed their desires of an accommodation, we know no farther than the common report.

On Thursday last the Bishop of Exeter kissed the King's hand, in order to be Archbishop of York, and the Bishop of Bristol* to be Bishop of Exeter.

A bill was brought to the Grand Jury against Captain Lexham, for dispersing the Prince of

* Sir Jonathan Trelawney.

Orange's Declarations, but would not find it, as is reported, unless they had a sight of a copy thereof.

One Mr. Purefoy is taken into custody of a messenger, and a lieutenant in the Lord Dartmouth's regiment is brought back.

On Thursday evening we were not a little surprised that part of some regiments had deserted to the enemy.

His Majesty departed this day, and lies at Windsor to-night, to-morrow at Basingstoke, and will be at Salisbury on Monday.

The ten officers taken in the Dutch fly-boat, were removed from the Gatehouse to Newgate.

This day the Queen, with the Prince of Wales, removed to Windsor.

The gentleman that writes the news, being called this day about extraordinary business, has been forced to leave the collection of the news to his clerk.

For John Ellis, Secretary to the Commissioners for the Revenue of Ireland,   At Dublin.

CCXXV.

Reports from Wales, and from the Dutch Army.—Foreign news.—Lord Delamere.

London, Nov. 20th, 1688.

SIR,

THOUGH it be commonly and credibly reported that our fleet sailed by Dover on Friday, and by Portsmouth on Saturday last, yet there is no manner of account yet come upon what design it was bent ; but all conclude it was with orders to find out the Dutch fleet, which is still about Torbay. But the sharp east winds we have had these three days, have been one reason that we have heard of no action.

His Majesty lay on Saturday at Windsor, and on Sunday night at Andover, and was expected yesterday betimes at Salisbury.

Here is a report as if Sir Rowland Gwynne were landed with a party in Wales, where he hopes to find those that will join him in great numbers ; but some think he has not experience sufficient in military affairs as to make it very probable.

We hear the Militia are every where strict in examining such as pass and traverse the country, especially if the persons or their numbers be any thing suspicious.

It is said his Majesty hath sent orders for the breaking down the bridge of Kensham, near Bristol, to prevent the incursion of the rebels into Glostershire.

His Royal Highness the Prince of Wales went from St. James's on Saturday, in his way, it is believed, towards Portsmouth. The Queen continues still at Whitehall, but will follow, as people say, in a few days.

The Dutch army is reported to begin to want money, yet the strictness of discipline keeps the soldiers in quiet. The Prince is said to have hanged one for stealing a bone of mutton, yet we do not hear any correction was given those that robbed the King's party of their horses and clothes.

We hear the French troops are drawing towards the water side in great numbers, and that Marshal de Humieres* is ordered that way from Flanders to command them, and to prevent any attempt the Dutch may make upon their coast.

The Dutch have offered their mediation between the Emperor and the Turks, but the first seems not inclined to a peace, but to pursue his conquests in Greece, and pretends to be able to send an army both to the Rhine and to the Danube against the French as well as the Turks. But the Imperial Court is too near akin to the Spanish to make any haste ; all the Palatinate being already gone, and in the power of the French, before the Emperor could resolve to write a letter, and promise his assistance.

The petition presented on Saturday by the Archbishops and other Lords,† (about nineteen)

* Lewis de Crevan, Marshal d'Humieres.   Created a Marshal of France in 1668 ; died in 1694.

† The Lords were, the two Archbishops, the Bishops of Norwich, St. Asaph, Ely, Peterborough, and Rochester ; Dukes of Grafton and Ormonde ; Earls of Dorset, Clare,

is printed. The prayer of it is, that his Majesty would forthwith call a free Parliament, and use such means as should to him seem fit for preventing the effusion of Christian blood.

A report is very hot about town, that the Lord Delamere is up in Cheshire, at the head of a considerable body of Horse; that he declared himself in favour of the Prince of Orange's proceedings, and had himself read that Prince's Declaration at the Market-Cross; those rumours adding at the same time the names of sundry lords and gentlemen that concur with that lord in the same measures, and that their general rendezvous is to be at Derby. But though several expresses are dispatched upon this account, yet, as all this is with uncertainty, we shall forbear all particulars till farther confirmation.

For John Ellis, Esq. Secretary to the
   Commissioners for the Revenue of
   Ireland,   At Dublin.

Clarendon, Burlington, Anglesey, and Rochester; the Lords Newport, Paget, Chandos, and Ossulston.

CCXXVI.

Storms at sea.—False reports.—Lord Thomas Howard.—
Prince of Orange at Bridgewater, &c.

London, Nov. 22d, 1688.

SIR,

THE winds have continued so loud and
violent of late, that we could not expect to hear
of any action between the fleets, were they both
never so well disposed ; besides, we are told
the Dutch fleet is dispersed by the late storm,
above thirty sail being driven to the westward
towards Land's end. His Majesty's fleet rides
bewestwards of Portsmouth, not many leagues
from Torbay.

We want the confirmation of the news that
is spread about, as if there had happened a ren-
contre betwixt a party of his Majesty's army,
and that of the Prince of Orange, and that
Colonel Kirk and some others were killed ; nor
do we find it to be true, what is said of Mr.
Bernard Howard's being killed in a duel by
one of his own officers, who had provoked Mr.

Howard to give him some unbecoming language.

His Majesty is in good health at Sarum, and reviews some part of his troops daily, who are cheerful and brisk. The Marshal de Schomberg threatened to bring most of them to their night-caps, without striking a stroke.

People please themselves here with a conceit as if Admiral Herbert had met with a French squadron, and had at one dash sunk nine or ten of them; which is every whit as true as that an army of 50,000 French are already landed at Dover.

Though there never was more occasion of inquiry for busy impertinent people, that gad about all day long for coffee and news; yet never was less certainty of what passes in the world, most people affecting to disguise the truth, and there being at present about this City many engines that are made use of to spread what most suits the humour of some party; yet the City of London was never more quiet, every man minding his business and securing their debts, and the generality of the soberer and the richer sort have expressed their dislike of these proceedings, which are like to perpetuate and entail war upon the nation, by the removal of the Prince of Wales, who is now at Portsmouth, and, as some will have it, will pass into France.

We have no farther account of the Lord Delamere and others in and about Cheshire, who are said to march out of that county to join others about Staffordshire and Nottinghamshire, in order to march to the West. It is a long march, and accidents may happen in the way. We do not yet hear of Sir Rowland Gwynne.

Our foreign advices tell us the Lord Thomas Howard* was come away from Rome,

* Lord Thomas Howard was the second son of Henry sixth Duke of Norfolk. In 1686, he was made Master of the Robes to James the Second. He was a Roman Catholic, and was in consequence sent ambassador to Rome in 1688. He adhered to James in his misfortunes, and went with him to Ireland: returning from whence to France, on his royal mas-

carrying with him, among other things, the Pope's Bull, whereby he submits all the differences between him and France to his Majesty's determination and mediation.

The French are fortifying all the places they have taken in the Palatinate, and are a-drawing together a considerable army to be ready against spring, in order to invade Holland. In the mean time, all hostilities are committed by sea and land by prizes and reprizes between those two nations.

The Prince of Orange has been at Bridgewater, and other places in the neighbourhood, and swept away all the horses in the county, haunting all the markets, and seizing all the cattle that come in, but giving some money for them. He took away a hundred in one market day at Tiverton, and borrowed seven from Sir Creswell Tint, a gentleman of that neighbourhood. We do not yet hear of his advancing

ter's affairs, he was lost at sea, Nov. 9th, 1689. His eldest son, Thomas, became eighth Duke of Norfolk, upon the death of his uncle Henry the seventh Duke, in 1701.

farther. It is said he has turned out the Corporation of Exon, and granted them a new Charter. He has also settled three Commissioners to manage the revenue of customs, excise, and hearth-money, who are Lord Wiltshire, Will. Harbord, the late Surveyor-general, and Monmouth's Anthony Rowe.

It is said, he and his Council have again published another Declaration, which is not yet seen in these parts, offering to be confined with his army to any corner of the kingdom, till a free Parliament be called. But this is but a hearsay.

For John Ellis, Esq. Secretary to the
   Commissioners for the Revenue of
   Ireland,   At Dublin.

CCXXVII.

The Declaration* of the Nobles, Gentry, and Commons, at their rendezvous at Nottingham.

Nov. 22nd, 1688.

WE the Nobles, Gentry, and Commons of these Northern countries assembled together at Nottingham for the defence of our laws, liberties, and properties, (according to these free-born liberties and privileges descended to us from our ancestors, the undoubted birth-right of the subjects of this kingdom of England,) not doubting but the infringers and invaders of our rights will represent us to the rest of the nation in the most malicious dress

---

* This was the declaration of the nobility and gentry of the neighbouring counties, who had been collected at Nottingham by the activity and influence of the Lords Devonshire and Delamere. Reresby, in his Memoirs, mentions their *rising* at this time. "Nov. 24th. We had now news from Nottingham, that the Earl of Devonshire, Lord Delamere, and many more noblemen and gentlemen were risen also in those parts, and that great numbers flocked in to them."

hey can put upon us, do here unanimously hink it our duty to declare to the rest of our persuasion and fellow-subjects the grounds of our undertakings.

We therefore, being by innumerable grievances made sensible that the very fundamentals of our liberty, religion, and properties, are about to be rooted out by our late Jesuitical Privy Council, as hath been of late too apparent—

1st, By the King's dispensing all established laws at his pleasure ;

2nd, By displacing all officers in any places of trust or advantage, and placing in their rooms known Papists deservedly made incapable of the same by the established laws of our land ;

3rd, By destroying the charters of most Corporations in the land ;

4th, By discouraging all persons that are not Papists, and preferring such as would turn Papists ;

5th, By displacing all honest and conscientious Judges, unless they would, contrary to their consciences, declare that to be law which was merely arbitrary ;

6th, By branding all men with the name of Rebels, that but offered to justify the law in a legal course against the arbitrary proceedings of the King, or any of his corrupt Ministers ;

7th, By burthening the nation with an army, to maintain the violation of the right of the subject ;

8th, By discountenancing the established reformed religion ;

9th, By forbidding the subjects the benefit of petitioning, and construing the same libellous, so rendering the laws a nose of wax to further their arbitrary ends; and many more too long here to insert :—

We, being thus made sadly sensible of the arbitrary and tyrannical Government that is by the influences of Jesuitical counsel coming upon us, do unanimously declare, that being not willing to deliver over our posterity to such conditions of Popery and slavery as the aforesaid oppressions inevitably threaten, we will, to the utmost of our power, oppose the same ; and by joining with the Prince of Orange, whom we hope God Almighty hath sent to rescue us from the oppressions aforesaid, will use our utmost endeavours for the recovery of our almost ruined laws, liberties, and religion ; and herein we hope all good Protestants and subjects will, with their lives and fortunes, be assistants to us, and not be bugbeared with the opprobrious term of Rebels, by which they would fright us to become perfect slaves to their tyrannical insolencies and usurpations ; for we assure ourselves that no rational unbiassed person will adjudge it rebellion to defend our laws and religion, which all our just Princes have sworn to maintain at their coronations ; which oath, how well it hath been observed, we desire a free Parliament may have the consideration of. We own it rebellion to resist our King that governs by law ; but he was always accounted a tyrant that made his will the law. To resist such an one, we justly esteem it no rebellion, but a necessary defence ; and in this confidence we doubt not of all honest Englishmen's assistance ; and humbly hope for and implore the great God's protection, that turneth the hearts of his people as pleaseth him best ; it having been observed that people can never be of one mind without his inspiration, which hath in all ages confirmed that observation— *Vox populi, vox Dei.* The present restoring of charters, and reversing the oppressive and unjust judgments on Magdalen College Fellows, &c. it is plain they are given, as plums are to children, but to still the people by deceiving them for a while. But if they then by this stratagem be fooled till this present storm that threatens the Papists be past, as soon as they shall be re-settled, the former oppressions will be put on with the greater vigour. But we hope, vain is the net that is spread in the sight of the birds ; for, first, the Papists' old rule—that faith is not to be kept with heretics, —and so they term Protestants, though the Popish religion is the greatest heresy ; secondly, and Queen Mary's observing her promises to the Suffolkmen that helped her to the crown; thirdly, and above all, the Pope's dispensing with breach of oaths, treaties, or promises, at his pleasure, when it makes for the service of Holy Church, as they call it : these, we say, are such convincing reasons to hinder us from giving credit to the aforesaid mock shows of redress, that we think ourselves bound in conscience to rest on no security that shall not be approved by a free elected Parliament, to whom, under God, we refer our cause.

CCXXVIII.

Battle expected to take place on Salisbury Plain.—Defections to the Prince of Orange.

London, Nov. 23rd, 1688.

I HAD your's of the 23rd past, and thank you, in the name of the kingdom, for the quiet repose you promised us this winter. But by the last easterly wind you would find we are not to enjoy such sweet sleeps as you wish us ; for the army, 27,000 strong, will be able to offer

battle by Tuesday next, on Salisbury Plains,
and our Imperial Monarch at the head of them,
where my person, amongst his faithful subjects,
intends to stick by him.   I am like to be well
paid for my pains, but cannot at this instant
tell the value : but it is no part of the reason
of my going; though I can to my sorrow say,
why milch-asses are provided; for the King's
health is in a very ill state, what with the
fatigue of these preparations, and the anguish
of such a sort of people's going to the enemy ;
viz. we are well assured of the Earls Wilshire,
Shrewsbury, Macclesfield, Lord Lorne, Mordant, Mr. Sydney, &c. ; we fear Earls Devon,*
Exeter,† Radnor,‡ Lord Lumley,‖ Lovelace,

* William (Cavendish), afterwards first Duke of Devonshire.

† John (Cecil) fifth Earl of Exeter.   He had married the
sister of Lord Devonshire, which probably led to his joining
the Prince of Orange : at all events, after the revolution, he
refused to take the oaths to William, and consequently lived
in retirement till his death, in 1700.

‡ Charles Bodville (Robartes) second Earl of Radnor,
grandson of John the first Earl.   He died 1723, s. p.

‖ Richard Viscount Lumley, in Ireland, created by

Earl Manchester,* Lord Grey,† Rutland,‡ with eighty gentlemen, and a great number of the

Charles the Second, Baron of Lumley Castle in Durham, and by William, Viscount Lumley of Lumley Castle, and Earl of Scarborough. He concurred zealously in the Revolution, and was very active, in conjunction with Lords Devonshire and Danby, in disposing the north of England favourably for the Prince of Orange. He also secured the town of Newcastle for the Prince's interest. After the Revolution, he served with William during his campaigns in Flanders ; and during his reign and the succeeding ones received many marks of royal favour. He died Dec. 17th, 1721. As Lord Lumley, he had distinguished himself at the battle of Sedgemoor ; and was the person who after the battle discovered and took prisoner the unhappy Duke of Monmouth.

* Charles (Montagu) fourth Earl and first Duke of Manchester. He had been some time previously in Holland with the Prince of Orange ; and upon the news of his landing, he raised a considerable body of horse in Huntingdonshire, and thereby secured that county to him. He was afterwards employed on various embassies, and was finally, by George the First, created Duke of Manchester, in 1719. He died 1722.

† Ford Lord Grey of Werk.

‡ John (Manners) ninth Earl and first Duke of Rutland. He was raised to the latter honour in 1703, and died 1711. He was divorced from his first wife, Anne Pierrepont, eldest daughter and coheiress of Henry Marquis of Dorchester,—a circumstance which, though apparently of small moment in

finest horses of England.   Our intelligence
from the West comes slow, or is much con-

itself, occasioned, according to Burnet, much caballing and
intrigue, from the period at which it happened, namely, the
reign of Charles the Second :—

"An accident happened at that time (1668), that made
the discoursing of those matters (i. e. the putting away of
the Queen) the common subject of discourse.   The Lord
Roos, afterwards Earl of Rutland, brought proofs of adul-
tery against his wife, and obtained a sentence of divorce
in the spiritual court : which amounting only to a separa-
tion from bed and board, he moved for a bill dissolving
the bond, and enabling him to marry another wife.   The
Duke of York and all his party apprehended the consequences of a parliamentary divorce ; so they opposed this
with great heat : and almost all the Bishops were of that
side ; only Cosins and Wilkins, the Bishops of Durham and
Chester, were for it.   And the King was as earnest in the setting it on, as the Duke was in opposing it.   The zeal which the
two brothers expressed on that occasion, made all people conclude that they had a particular concern in the matter.   The
bill passed ; and upon that precedent, some moved the
King that he would order a bill to be brought in to divorce
him from the Queen.   This went so far, that a day was
agreed on for making the motion in the House of Commons,
as Mr. May of the Privy Purse told me.   But he added,
when he told me of this design, that three days before the
motion was to be made, the King called for him, and told
him that matter must be let alone, for it would not do."

cealed. The end of these matters is dreadful, or at least the execution. This household went to-day; and we think the King may before, or on Monday.

If I should repeat all the occurrences that pass here, they would fill volumes. But the ordinary people list themselves apace, and the gentry thereabouts are slow in coming in; but those of the East make up the want sufficiently. The Duke of Grafton is here, though calumniated, and some others; none can be absent two days but undergoes censure. Lord Colchester,* Thomas Wharton,†

* Richard (Savage) Lord Colchester, eldest son of Richard third Earl Rivers, whom he succeeded in his honours in 1694. He was employed during the reigns of William and Anne, both in a military and diplomatic capacity; and in 1712 he succeeded the Duke of Marlborough as Master-General of the Ordnance, during the disgrace at Court of that eminent man. He died the same year.

† *Thomas Wharton* must mean Thomas Lord Wharton, afterwards created by Queen Anne Marquis of Malmesbury and Wharton. Burnet mentions him as one of the first who joined the Prince of Orange.

Y 2

Charles Godfrey,* Anthony Roe, &c. are gone, I fear.

For John Ellis, Esq. Secretary of His
    Majesty's Revenue in Ireland,
Ireland.   Dublin.

CCXXIX.

Reports from the West.—The King expected at Salisbury.—
Samuel Ellis gone away.—Prince of Wales gone to France.
—Skirmishes, &c.

London, Nov. 24th, 1688.

SIR,

THE Falmouth letters of the 19th instant say the company of foot of the Earl of
Huntingdon's regiment, that was in Pendennis Castle, has marched towards Plymouth,
and a company of the Militia marched in; to
which are to be added three companies more of
the Militia, who are to relieve each other. The

* Colonel Charles Godfrey, Master of the Jewel Office, and
husband of Arabella Churchill, the mistress of James the
Second.

Earl of Bath hath made Sir Joseph Tredenham, Sir Peter Killigrew, Sir Vyell Vivian,* and Colonel Trevanian as Governors of Pendennis.

Last week a great tinwork gave over, by which four hundred tinners are out of employ, who, it is feared, will all march to the Prince of Orange. None yet of the county of Cornwall are come into him.

In the western parts reports have been of a massacre in Ireland of 6000 ; but a vessel is come into Falmouth, which came out of Cork the last week : the master says, that all was in peace and quiet, and no such thing feared.

On Saturday came into Falmouth road a stout ship, supposed a Dutch man-of-war : she came in with all her colours flying, and had a shot for not striking.

The Prince hath seized Dartmouth Castle, and is marched eastwards.

Yesterday and this day the officers in the Tower of London have been employed in plant-

* Sir Vyell Vyvyan, Bart. of Trelowarren, in Cornwall.

ing mortars upon the White Tower, which makes a noise among the women and children, &c.

On Tuesday morning the King intended to rendezvous his whole army on the plain next Salisbury; and it is generally believed the army was then drawn up. But I have not seen any letters thence.

It is generally said, the advanced guards of both armies have had some sharp rencounters, and many men killed on both sides.

Notwithstanding what hath been so positively reported and written of the Honourable Bernard Howard's being killed, it proves a mistake. And also that of Colonel Kirk's being cut in pieces by his own men as they marched for Salisbury, in Popham-lane.

Mr. Ellis,* (brother to the Popish Bishop,) late sworn Marshal of the King's Bench, having, as is said, got some thousands of unfortunate gentlemen under his custody, yesterday morning took occasion to move all things

* Samuel Ellis.

out of his chamber, and withdrew. And the same day the Judges of the King's Bench did admit into that office one Mr. Philpott, an attorney, who was accordingly sworn in Court.

This day it is the current discourse that his Highness the Prince of Wales, the Countess of Powis governess, Madam Labardy the dry-nurse, Father Peters, &c., are safely arrived from Portsmouth to Dieppe in France.*

This day came forth a Proclamation dated at Salisbury the 22nd instant, and gives pardon to all, without exception, with the Prince of Orange, &c.

The Prince hath left 4000 horse and foot in garrison at Exeter, and made Mr. Seymour,† the late Speaker, Governor.

The King's Majesty hath been a little indis-

---

* This report was premature. The Queen and Prince of Wales stayed in England till the 9th of December, and Petre fled only a day or two sooner.

† Sir Edward Seymour, Bart, the third baronet of that name. He was descended from one of the sons of the Protector Somerset by his first wife, whom he cruelly disinherited, both with regard to title and estate, in favour of his

posed, and some drops of blood fell from his nose;* upon which his Majesty was let blood, and now is perfectly well.

sons by his second wife. This younger branch ended in the proud Duke of Somerset, and the title of Somerset consequently reverted to the grandson of Sir Edward. Sir Edward was a public man of considerable eminence, and had been Speaker of the House of Commons, from which situation the Court rejected him, for his enmity to Popery, and also to Lord Danby, who was then minister. An old lampoon of the time attributes this measure entirely to that lord.

> " 'Cause Seymour to be Speaker is
> The fittest man that can be,
> He therefore now rejected is
> By Thomas Earl of Danby."

Seymour was generally on the patriotic side, but his integrity was suspected from the places he got for himself. " He was a graceful man, bold and quick. But he had a sort of pride so peculiar to himself, that I never saw any thing like it. He had neither shame nor decency with it. He was violent against the Court till he forced himself into good posts."—Burnet.

He was one of the first who joined the Prince, and advised the signing an agreement or association to keep people together. " The Prince," adds Burnet, " put Devonshire and Exeter under Seymour's government, who was Recorder of Exeter; and he advanced with his army, leaving a small garrison there."

* James's illness and bleeding of the nose is mentioned by

A council of war, held at Salisbury, resolved it
was his Majesty's interest to return to London
with the army, lest the Prince in his march
get betwixt the King and his capital city.
To which his Majesty hath consented ; and, I
am told, the army is upon their march, and
that the King, who was expected this night,
will be here on Monday at the farthest.

A small party of foot being far advanced
towards the King's forces, Colonel Sarsefield
commanded a detached party of horse and
dragoons, and met with them at Wincanton,
eighteen miles from Salisbury, where the colonel killed about thirty, and hanged four, and
lost of his own party five, and Colonel Webb's

Reresby, Burnet, Lord Clarendon, and Sir Patrick Hume.
Burnet says, "his blood was in such a fermentation, that
he was bleeding much at the nose, which returned oft
upon him every day." And Sir Patrick Hume's Diary
thus mentions it :—" Monday, 19th November, King
James came to Salisbury. Tuesday, viewing the plains on
horseback to choose a camp, he fell in excessive bleeding
at the nose, was four times let blood that week, and parted
toward London on Saturday the 24th."

son, who was a cornet. But it is said young Schombergh* meeting a party of the King's horse upon Doncaster† road, hath killed fifty-three out of sixty-five in revenge, refusing to give quarter, as is by report charged upon Colonel Sarsefield, besides the hanging four, which some say were revolters.

The King's fleet are at Portsmouth now: some have suffered much in the late storms, and I am told a fourth-rate is lost.

Just now comes an express that the Earl of Danby and some lords have seized York,

---

* Meinhardt Schombergh, second son of the first Duke of that name—created Duke of Leinster in Ireland, in 1691 ; succeeded his elder brother, Frederick, who was killed at the battle of Marsaglia in Piedmont, in the English Dukedom of Schombergh, in 1693. He died without male issue in 1719, and his titles extinguished with him. Burnet observes, "The Duke of Schombergh was a better officer in the field than in the cabinet ; he did not enough know how to prepare for a campaign ; he was both too inactive and too haughty." He was, however, without doubt, a man of bravery and merit.

† This must be a mistake, as there is no place of this name in the West of England.

the governor, and castle, and declared for the Prince of Orange.*

(No address on this Letter.)

CCXXX.

24th Nov. 1688.

WE have no good news here, nor any thing from beyond sea. The King and his army return next week from Sarum. The Prince of Orange is said to be in full march this way. Yorke city is seized by the Earl of Danby, his sons, and associates. God knows what will next follow !

For John Ellis, Esq. Secretary
for the Revenue of Ireland,
At Dublin.

---

* Reresby gives a long account of this transaction. He was Governor of York for King James, and Lord Danby and the others seem to have completely overreached him. The principal actors in the affair appear, under Lord Danby, to have been, Sir Henry Goodrick, Lord Lumley, Lord Haughton, Lord Willoughby of Eresby, and Mr. Trenchard.

CCXXXI.

Prince of Orange at Wincanton.—Petitions for a free Parliament, &c.—Mr. Leveson Gower's house plundered.—Duke of St. Alban's regiment.

London, Nov. 24th, 1688.

SIR,

WE had most violent storms these three nights past, which still began with the evenings, and must have done great damage to the fleets ; though we have not yet the particulars of it : two or three of his Majesty's ships are already put into Porstmouth to be refitted, and the Lord Dartmouth got in time enough to avoid the brunt of the hurricane.

It is said the Prince of Orange is marched with his artillery out of Exeter, and takes his way towards Axminster, and intends to encamp at a place called Wincanton, (where the late skirmish was, mentioned in the Gazette of this day,) though some think his chief aim is upon Bristol, and will make the best of his way hither, though the season and those roads be very inconvenient for heavy carriage and cannon.

Most people had difficulty to believe that the Prince of Orange had forbidden praying for the King; but letters from good hands are said to confirm it, and that Burnett's prayer for success against the King is commonly used, though the English clergy have refused it.

We are told of several addresses and petitions for a free Parliament that are coming from several parts of the kingdom; but we are told the generality of England, as well as this city, do not intend to meddle with the merits of this invasion, but to take a surer card, and to declare for the Monarchy, and our laws as now established. The gentry of Yorkshire* were assembled for that purpose on Thursday last, the result of whose deliberations we shall know ere long.

* The Declaration from York (which, as Reresby informs us was signed by, " Lords, six ; Lords' sons, three ; Baronets, five ; Knights, six ; Esquires and Gentlemen, sixty-six; and Citizens of York, fifty-six,") was for a free Parliament, &c.

We did not trouble the reader with a copy of the petition the Bishops and other Lords delivered to the King, which has been printed with the pretended answer the King thought fit to give them ; for that certainly the one if not both were false and contrived to amuse the people ; but the true one may be seen in the Gazette, whereby the cheat of the other may better appear.

Of all the men that have appeared in arms and declared for the Prince, none have done more zealously than those who began the dance in Cheshire, who gather weight like a snow-ball, and, as many affirm, do plunder as they go ; having begun with the taking of a waggon of arms sent hence to one Captain Lee's company quartered at Manchester.   But we must suspend our belief to what is nevertheless confidently reported, namely, that they fall foul upon their old friends and neighbours, particularly Mr. Lewson Gore,* whose house they are said

* William Leveson Gower, who afterwards, upon the death of his nephew Sir Thomas Gower, Bart. in 1689, suc-

o have entered by force, and taken away all
iis arms and horses, and even his lady's coach-
iorses, by reason the nice will condemn this
conduct as too outrageous a violation of the
rules of knight-errantry. The chief officers of
his body are affirmed to be old Oliverians that
iave long lain lurking about Chester and
Cheshire, in expectation of a day of plunder.

The party that was detached to break the
bridge of Kensham, near Bristol, was commanded by Captain Loyd, of the Earl of Peterborough's* regiment, who in his return met
seventeen sparks, well mounted, marching to
the West, and took nine of them prisoners,
and all their horse.

ceeded to the Baronetcy, and became the fourth Baronet of
this family.   He was the ancestor of the present Marquis of
Stafford.   He had been one of the Duke of Monmouth's bail,
in 1683, and was long member of Parliament for the borough
of Newcastle-under-Line.   He married Jane Granville, eldest
daughter of the Earl of Bath, and died in 1691.

* Henry Earl of Peterborough.   Sir John Guise had,
with the assistance of the inhabitants, obliged the Duke of
Beaufort to surrender the city of Bristol to the Prince's
interest.

His Majesty continues in good health at Sarum; only was let blood once since his being there.

Several of the Duke of St. Alban's regiment are come back, though in a most plundered condition, having refused the large pay and encouragement which was offered them, but it would not weigh against their allegiance.

For John Ellis, Esq. Secretary to the
Commissioners for the Revenue of
Ireland,   At Dublin.

CCXXXII.

The King returned to town.—Defections to the Prince of Orange.—Flight of the Princess of Denmark.—The Lords sent for to the King.

Nov. 27th, 1688.

YESTERDAY, between four and five of the clock, the King came to Whitehall, and looks very well. We hear by some of his company, that Prince George,* the Dukes of Graf-

* Lord Clarendon observes in his Diary :—" Nov. 26th. I met Lord Preston, who told me, that on Saturday night, at

ton and Ormonde, Lord Churchill,* Lord
Drumlanrick,† Sir George Hewitt,‡ Colonel
Andover, after the King was gone to bed, Prince George,
the Duke of Ormonde, Lord Drumlanrig, and Mr. H. Boyle,
went back to the Prince of Orange." To this passage the
following note is appended :—" They had supped with the
King the same evening. Prince George left a letter for
James, (which may be seen in *Kennet's History of England*,)
excusing his own conduct and blaming the unhappy Monarch. The Prince had been accustomed, when he heard of
the defection of any of those who had been obliged to the
King, to say, ' *Est-il possible ?*' The only remark James
made upon the Prince's flight, was ' Is *Est-il possible* gone
too ?' In King James's Memoirs it is said, ' He was more
troubled at the unnaturalness of the action, than the want of
his service, for that the loss of a good trooper had been of
greater consequence.' But when, on his return to London,
he heard that the Princess Anne had fled, under pretence of
avoiding his displeasure, he burst into tears, and exclaimed,
' God help me ! my own children have forsaken me.' "

* John Duke of Marlborough.

† James (Douglas) Earl of Drumlanrig, eldest son of William first Duke of Queensberry in Scotland, whom he succeeded as second Duke of Queensberry in 1695. He was
the manager of the Union between England and Scotland,
for which service Queen Anne made him Duke of Dover in
England, and showered upon him places, pensions, and
patronage. He died in 1711.

‡ Sir George Hewitt was in the Princess of Denmark's
household.

Trelawney,* Colonel Berkeley,† Lieutenant-General Kirke, Mr. Harry Boyle,‡ Captain Kendall, and very many others of note, are gone to the Prince of Orange's army. Kirke, we hear, is retaken by the King's forces, and bringing to town; but what is at least as bad news as this, is, that yesterday morning, when the Princess of Denmark's women went to take her out of her bed, they found she had withdrawn herself, and hath not yet been heard of; nobody went in her company that

* Trelawney was an officer of reputation, and was the brother of Sir Jonathan Trelawney, Bart. Bishop of Bristol. Burnet says it was he who engaged the Bishop to be favourable to the Revolution.

† Colonel John Berkeley, afterwards Viscount Fitzharding in Ireland. He and his wife were both in the household of the Prince and Princess of Denmark.

‡ Henry Boyle, second son of Richard first Earl of Burlington. He was Secretary of State and Chancellor of the Exchequer during the reign of Queen Anne; and was created by George the First, Baron Carleton, of Carleton, in the county of York. He died unmarried in 1725, and bequeathed his house in Pall Mall, called Carleton House, to Frederick, Prince of Wales.

we hear of, besides Lady Churchill * and Mrs. Berkeley.† Lord Churchill's bed-cham-

---

* Afterwards, Sarah Duchess of Marlborough.

† " Nov. 26th, Monday. As I was walking in Westminster-hall, on a sudden was a rumour all about, that the Princess was gone away, nobody knew whither; that somebody had violently carried her away. I went presently to the Cockpit. I found my Lady Frecheville and all the women in great consternation. All the light I could get was, that last night, after her Royal Highness was in bed, the chamber-doors locked, and Mrs. Danvers in bed in the outer-room, where she used to lie when in waiting, she rose again, went down the back-stairs, and accompanied only by Lady Churchill, Mrs. Berkeley, and a maid of Lord Churchill's, went into a coach and six horses, which stood ready at the street gate. This was all I could learn."—Diary of Henry Earl of Clarendon.

" The Princess went to bed at the usual time to prevent suspicion. I came to her soon after ; and by the back-stairs which went down from her closet, her Royal Highness, my Lady Fitzharding, and I, with one servant, walked to the coach, where we found the Bishop ‡ and the Earl of Dorset. They conducted us that night to the Bishop's house in the City, and the next day to my Lord Dorset's at Copt-hall. From thence we went to the Earl of Northampton's, and from

---

‡ Of London.

ber place is given to Lord Melford,* and his troop of Guards to the Duke of Berwick ; and it is said this morning that Lord Dover hath the government of Portsmouth, and Mr. Skelton is made Lieutenant of the Tower. We hear to-day that the Duke of Albemarle is dead at Jamaica. The King hath sent to all the Lords Spiritual and Temporal that are about the town, to attend him this afternoon, at four of the clock ; if I hear any thing that passes there, you shall have it. I have told you many lamentable stories, and I wish you do not hear more from other people. I thank you for your favour of the 5th of this month, and for the good account you give me of yourself.

thence to Nottingham, where the country gathered about the Princess ; nor did she think herself safe, till she saw that she was surrounded by the Prince of Orange's friends."—Duchess of Marlborough's Apology.

" In a little while a small army was formed about the Princess, who chose to be commanded by the Bishop of London, of which he too easily accepted."—Burnet, Hist. of his own Time.

* Drummond Earl of Melfort, younger brother of the Earl of Perth.

Remember us to my brother and sister, when
you see them. I do not write to-night to either
of them : all here are your servants. Pray, tell
me what is become of Dr. Dunn. I hope you
have heard I have delivered the inclosed you
sent me for Lord Clarendon. I am always,

Dear Sir,

Yours most faithfully.

We hear that the Lords have spoken very
freely to his Majesty. The things proposed by
them were a free Parliament, a general pardon,
and a Treaty. The King hath taken a short
time to consider of them, when they are to
attend him again.*

For John Ellis, Esq. Secretary to the
    Commissioners of His Majesty's
    Revenues of Ireland,
Dublin.

----

* The Lords who attended the King's summons were about
forty in number : of these, Lords Oxford, Godolphin, Falcon-
berg, Rochester, Clarendon, Halifax, and Nottingham, and
the Lord Chancellor, were the persons who took the principal

CCXXXIII.

Duke of Ormonde gone to the Prince of Orange.—Commissioners sent to the Prince.—Private business.

Dec. 1st, 1688.

DEAR FRIEND,

I AM very much obliged to you for your very good opinion of me. I wish heartily you were a Duke, I would as faithfully serve you as I did my old master,* for above twenty-eight years. I thank God, I defy any man that ever I dealt with, that can say I ever got sixpence of them, as being partial, but paid when I knew there was the most necessity. I do

part in the discussion. Lord Clarendon appears to have spoken with great boldness. (See a long account of the interview in his Diary.) After having heard them, the King sent them away, with the following words:—" My Lords, I have heard you all: you have spoken with great freedom, and I do not take it ill of any of you. I may tell you I will call a Parliament; but for the other things you have proposed, they are of great importance, and you will not wonder that I take one night's time to consider of them."

* The first Duke of Ormonde.

wish all prosperity to his present Grace. He went with the Prince of Denmark to the Prince of Orange, who is not dead of a fever; quite the contrary. People say there is a trumpeter sent to know if Commissioners will have access; and if they may, then Lord Halifax, Lord Nottingham, and Lord Godolphine will be sent. This is the common talk, and there is a proclamation for a free Parliament, and mentions a general pardon. God, I hope, will end this in a peace, and the King and kingdom's welfare. I know you will get the licences as cheap and for as long as you can; it is hardly worth the charge, for my cousin Nobbs will tell you, that the last half-year for Mr. Douglas and I comes but to 20l. 1s. 6d. My constable's places are no more for a year. I hope it is not as dear as those that have thousands, but we must submit; if things be a little settled, I intend to come in the spring. I am sorry to hear that people cannot leave the kingdom without charge. You have news enough, so I write none. All in St. James's send service to you.   I am at the next house, when you find time.   It is thought others have taken their leave, and said nothing.

Adieu.

For John Ellis, Esq. Secretary to the
    Commissioners of His Majesty's
    Revenue of Ireland,

At Dublin.

CCXXXIV.

Queen and Prince of Wales gone to France.——The King gone also.——Prince of Orange at Oxford.—Papists put out.—— Burning of a Popish Chapel.—Prince of Orange's answer.

Dec. the 11th, 1688.

DEAR FRIEND,

I AM to give you a thousand thanks for your's of the 23d of November.   As to the licences, if they are but for three months, I hope we may have some cheaper and for longer time.

I am now to tell you that the Queen and

Prince of Wales went down the River yesterday morning, and it is believed gone for France ; and the King went this morning about the same time,* I hear hardly any body with him. God preserve him in health ! but here all people are wondering. The Prince of Orange will be in Oxford this night. The people in the City are searching all Roman Catholic

* " The night between the 9th and 10th of December, the Queen, in disguise, crossed the Thames to Lambeth in an open boat, exposed to wind and rain. At Lambeth, under the walls of a church, she waited till a coach could be got ready in the next inn. She went from this to Gravesend, where she embarked with the Prince of Wales on a small vessel, which conveyed them safely to Calais, from whence she went to Versailles, where she was received by the King of France with great marks of affection, which was some alleviation to her melancholy situation. The King, being fully determined to follow the Queen, waited but one day to execute his design. The night between the 10th and 11th of December, in a plain suit and bob-wig, he took water at Whitehall, accompanied only by Sir Edward Hales and Ab-badie, a Frenchman, page of the back-stairs, without acquainting any other with his intention."—Rapin.

" As they passed the river, they flung the Great Seal into it, which was some months after found by a fisherman near Fox-Hall."—Burnet.

houses for arms and ammunition, and this day they are about the Strand and other places. The Duke of Northumberland has put out all Papists out of his troop of Guards; and so they say they will out of all the army.   The King's party, which I hear was Colonel Butler's dragoons, and the Prince's had a skirmish : it is said about fifty of the King's were killed. This was about Reading, on Saturday night or Sunday.   I am told a Common Council were called this night ; the Bishops and Lords that are . here sat at Guildhall to-day with my Lord Mayor, who is the best man in the King's absence ; and Colonel Skelton, who was Lieutenant of the Tower, came and yielded up his trust,* and for the present my Lord of Clare† and some other lords are in it.   This sort of news concerns every body ; but I now

* Lord Lucas was made Lieutenant of the Tower, in the place of Skelton.

† Gilbert (Holles) third Earl of Clare.   He took an active part in favour of the Revolution, which was the concluding scene of his life, as he died January 16th, 1689.

ell you that the good Lady Dowager of Ossory* died this morning about six o'clock. She was taken yesterday morning with a sort of an apoplectic fit, and had three or four of them ; and so that good lady is taken out of a world that is, and like to be, very full of trouble. The Prince seems to say he will settle Ireland ; if so, the Comptroller of the Ordnance was turned out without any cause. I pray consult Garrett and my cousin Gourny what is fit to be done. If that employment be in arrear in the Treasury, I wish an item were given not to pay. This night I was frightened with the wonderful light in the sky, and it was the rabble had gotten the wainscoat and seats

* Amelia of Nassau, daughter of Lewis of Nassau, the natural son of Maurice Prince of Orange. She married, in 1659, Thomas Earl of Ossory, eldest son of the first Duke of Ormonde, and was the mother by him of the second Duke, as well as of other children. Lord Ossory has left behind him as fair a fame as any man of his day, as well for virtue as for talent. Anthony à Wood says, in speaking of his conduct in battle, " *He gallantly acted beyond the fiction of a romance.*" His father's touching lamentation over him is well known. He died in 1680.

at a Popish chapel in Lincoln's Inn Fields, and
set it on fire in the middle of it. Till we
knew what it was, we guessed it to be a great
fire. Here a very great guard, both militia and
the army, you will hear very suddenly all declaring for the Prince of Orange; from whom
the Commissioners sent to the King, before he
went away, this message, that he came to settle
the Protestant religion, and desired all the Papists might be disbanded, and to call a Parliament; and that he would not come near London but with the King's leave, and with what
number of men the King should say, provided
he had not a greater to receive him; but now
it is believed he will be here very soon. My
wife, and all in St. James's, send hearty service
to you. I hope I may see you in the spring.
God send us a good meeting!

For John Ellis, Esq. Secretary to the
    Commissioners of the Revenue of
    Ireland, at the Custom-House,
                    In Dublin.

CCXXXV.

Dutch officers released.—Address to the Prince of Orange.—
Riots in London.—Chancellor attempts to escape, and is
taken.—General news.

London, Dec. 13th, 1688.

SIR,

UPON notice on Tuesday of the King's being secretly withdrawn, the English-Dutch officers that were under confinement in the Savoy were discharged, and are now gone to attend the Prince.

The same day, in the morning, the Countess Dowager of Ossory departed this life, at the Duke of Ormond's house, in St. James's Square.

In our last we left the Lords assembled, as also the Common Council for this City. The former have departed, the Bishop of Ely, the Lords Pembroke, Weymouth, Culpepper,* &c. to wait on the Prince; and the latter, four Aldermen and eight Commoners, to carry his

* Thomas second Lord Colepeper.

Highness an address and invitation to town ;
their names are Sir Wm. Pritchard, Sir Sam.
Dashwood, Sir Wm. Ashurst, and Sir Thom.
Stampe, the two Mr. Hublands, Mr. Ham-
mond, Mr. Langham, Mr. Box, Mr. Robinson,
Sir Ben. Newland, and *   :
A messenger being likewise dispatched to the
Lords in the North, to engage them to ap-
proach the town.

On Tuesday night there was an alarm, occasioned by burning the Papists' Lincoln's-Inn-
Fields chapel.   They did the like to the chapels of St. John's, Clerkenwell, and Lime-
street ; but not easily breaking into the latter,
cried, they would down with it, were it as
strong as Portsmouth.   And accordingly, having levelled them, they carried all the trumpery
in mock procession and triumph, with oranges
on the tops of swords and staves, with great
lighted candles in gilt candlesticks ; thus victo-
riously passing by the Guards that were drawn
up.   And after having bequeathed these trin-

* So in the original.

kets to the flames, they visited Harry Hill's Printing-house, which they served in like manner. But what is most ungrateful is, their execution reaching to the Spanish Ambassador's* house, which they plundered of all its rich furniture, plate, money, and three coaches, to the value, as is computed, of 20,000*l.* All sober people are extraordinarily concerned at this horrid violation of the law of nations; and the

* " Though, upon the King's flight, the militia of London and Westminster were immediately up in arms, they could not prevent the mob from assembling and committing some disorders. They confined their rage chiefly to the mass-houses erected by the King in the city and suburbs, which they demolished entirely, and made bonefires with the materials. And as there were also chapels in the houses of ambassadors, those of the Spanish and Florentine ambassadors were rifled, before a stop could be put to the disorder. In the first of these chapels the principal Court-Papists had conveyed all their valuable effects, and this probably was the chief cause of the pillage. The houses of the other ambassadors were preserved, by the great care of some Lords. The two ministers of Spain and Florence were afterwards largely recompensed for their losses."†—Rapin.

† The Spanish ambassador had seventeen thousand pounds for his losses.—Buckingham's Account of the Revolution.

Lords are said to have assured his Excellency that they will study some means to make him satisfaction.

Yet, however ill this has been resented, and whatever precaution could be used, they did the like yesterday evening to the Duke of Florence's Minister's house in the Hay Market. Nevertheless, the Trained Bands came up to disperse them, and a soldier discharging his musket at them, shot his officer (Captain Douglass) through the back.   This performance being over, they went to the Nuncio's,* who being flown, the landlord with some money compounded with them for the house.   The flame of this confusion still increasing, and the mobile threatening to treat the French and all other ambassadors' houses in like manner, the Council being then assembled, got a body of horse together, and ordering them to fire with ball, this gave a check to those disorders, though they seem still resolved to go thorough-stitch.

The King is said to have left a paper behind

* Dada.

him, directed to the Earl of Feversham, for him to disband the army ; which his Lordship read at the head of most regiments, and accordingly disbanded them, some with, others without their arms ; and it is dismal to think what will become of such vast numbers of poor wretches, if the Prince's mercy and the people's compassion be not extraordinary.*

In the mean while, the Lords Churchill and Colchester, now with the Prince, have sent to the troop of Guards to be in a body, and they will unite them in few days.

On Tuesday, in the afternoon, returned the three Commissioners that were sent to the Prince of Orange, bringing with them five proposals from his Highness for the accommodating the present differences, but were extremely concerned to find that the Prince's good incli-

---

* " Before the King went off, he writ to the Earl of Feversham to disband the army, without any care of their pay, probably on purpose to cause disturbances in the kingdom by the discontents of the officers and soldiers." Rapin.

nations and their good offices were rendered abortive by the King's being withdrawn.

We hear not yet what is become of their Majesties; but the King is said to have taken along with him those writs of elections that were not issued out, as also the Broad and Privy Seals, with the Crowns and Sceptres.

Yesterday, the Lord Chancellor, in a black wig, and other contrivances to disguise, offered a collier fifty guineas to carry him to Hamburgh. The mate, having seen him formerly, suspected who he was; and consulting with a merchant, he advised them to repair to the Lord Mayor for an order to seize him; but not meeting with satisfaction there, they repaired to the Council at Whitehall, and orders being accordingly given, he was taken and brought, amid universal execration of the people, before Lord Mayor; who, upon sight of the prisoner, fell into a violent paralytic fit, so as to hinder him from examining him, and still continues ill. Nevertheless, upon the directions of the Council at Whitehall, the Lord Chancellor was committed prisoner to the Tower.*

* " During these irruptions of the mob, Chancellor Jefferies, disguised in a seaman's habit, in order to escape in a vessel freighted for Hamburgh, was discovered, as he was looking out of the window of the house where he had concealed himself.   He was immediately seized by the mob, and, after many indignities put upon him, carried before the Lord Mayor, who declined meddling with him.   But the Chancellor, seeing himself in the hands of an enraged mob, which threatened to tear him in pieces, desired that he might be sent to the Tower, which at last was granted him, not as a favour, but in hopes of seeing him shortly conducted from thence to the gallows.   It is pretended, he offered to discover many secrets, and for that reason was kept some time in prison, till the affairs of the Government should be settled.   But he died in that interval by the blows he had received, according to some ; by drinking spirituous liquors, according to others ; and as some pretend, of the stone.   Never man had better deserved a public punishment, as an atonement for all the mischiefs done to his country, and for all the blood spilt by his means."—Rapin.

" Jefferies, finding the King was gone, saw what reason he had to look to himself ; and, apprehending that he was now exposed to the rage of the people, whom he had provoked with so particular a brutality, he had disguised himself to make his escape.   But he fell into the hands of some who knew him.   He was insulted by them with as much scorn

2 A 2

The Bishop of Chester* is said to have been seized near Dover; and Baron Jenner, Burton, and Graham, at the town of Fereham; Bishop Ellis† is also secured, and William Penn was brought before the Lords at Whitehall, who were prevailed upon to make 6000*l.* bail for him; and diligent search is made after such others as are reputed to have been injurious to the Government.

The Prince is expected in town to-morrow.

About two this morning an alarm was spread through City and suburbs of "Rise, arm, arm! the Irish are cutting throats;" insomuch that in half an hour's time there was an appearance of above 100,000 men to have

and rudeness as they could invent. And after many hours tossing him about, he was carried to the Lord Mayor, whom they charged to commit him to the Tower, which the Lord Lucas had then seized, and in it had declared for the Prince. The Lord Mayor was so struck with the terror of this rude populace, and with the disgrace of a man who had made all people tremble before him, that he fell into fits upon it, of which he died soon after."—Burnet.

* Thomas Cartwright.
† Philip Ellis.

made head against any enterprise of that nature : all the windows of the houses being lighted with candles from top to bottom. But these terrors were quickly over upon notice that the Prince of Orange's advance-guard was near the town.

This night came a letter from the King himself at Feversham, directing what servants he has in town to be to him thither, with fresh linen and clothes. Besides those that are stopped at that place, many are stopped at Dover.

The Duke of Grafton arrived this evening at Whitehall.

For John Ellis, Esq. Secretary for the
    Commissioners for the Revenue of
    Ireland,   At Dublin.

CCXXXVI.

Affairs of the Countess of Ossory. — Inquiries respecting
certain passages in the political life of Lord Ossory, &c.

King's Weston, 15th Dec. 1688.

SIR,

THE world can never be too busy to pay
acknowledgments. I did on the 22nd past
receive your long one of the 3rd, descanting
on what Mr. Mulys had writ, and with material observations in some points. But I cannot
think of this argument without condoling
with you the good Countess of Ossory's death,
who, it seems, ere Tuesday left this troublesome life.

I will write to Mr. Mulys to have those
commissions and letters from the King of
Spain, &c., which you say were left in her
Ladyship's hands. Your son and I may cast
an eye over them.

You promise to enlarge the relation of what

his Lordship* did in February 1677, when he went into Holland, which I am every day expecting; for it is dangerous to let a man's thoughts cool and pass to other things.

When my Lord went in Nov. 1674, about he match,† he had the single commission for t, and my Lord Arlington's affair was quite another thing. Nor had the Prince at that time any thoughts of the match; but when afterwards he had, as in 1677, and when Earl of Danby was in full power, it is possible, as you note, that Monsieur Benting being put over to the Duke of Ormond about it, might

* Sir Robert apparently was in the intention of writing a life of Lord Ossory, as this paragraph and the next relate to particulars in his career, respecting which he was anxious to be more particularly informed.

† Lord Ossory had been sent to Holland in 1674, to negotiate the marriage of the Prince of Orange with the Princess Mary; which however did not then take effect. It was renewed in 1677, and brought to a successful issue by the means of Lord Danby, who saw he could not maintain his ground as Minister, unless he withdrew the King from the French Alliance. In 1677, Lord Ossory served under the Prince of Orange at the siege of Charleroi.

for its success be referred to the Earl of Danby, who, indeed, did vigorously drive it on, and he had the popular applause of it.

You do not name to me that great man that opposed my Lord's design upon Helvoetsluyes, but I desire you would. And to send me as soon as you can whatever notes you think referable to this argument.

We are all here much concerned for the safety of our friends on your side. God send a happy conclusion of these matters.

I am ever, Sir,

Your most affectionate friend

and humble servant,

ROBERT SOUTHWELL.

For John Ellis, Esq. Secretary to His
Majesty's Revenue in Ireland,
        At Dublin.

CCXXXVII.

The King gone.—The Prince and Princess of Orange at Windsor.

London, Dec. 18th, 1688.

DEAR SIR,

YOURS of the 24th of the past month came hither, and I had it this evening upon my return hither in company. Your friend came well last night. As for the money, that will not be paid me. I will fetch it ere long, and possibly may get it with interest. I thank you for your care of your friend's reputation. I think his late behaviour hath wiped out all such like spots. The King, upon his withdrawing himself, was stopped in Kent, and conducted up hither; but this morning, by permission, went to Rochester, in order to proceed whither he pleased. God send all to end well! prudence will let me say no more. I should be glad to hear you were on this side, for many reasons. I have been some time out of town.

Prince and Princess of Denmark are at Windsor; come hither to-morrow. Prince of Orange has the sole dominion here; 1000 men in the Tower, and 6000 about his person at St. James's.

For John Ellis, Esq. Secretary of his
     Majesty's Revenue in Ireland,
                    Dublin.

CCXXXVIII.

The King returned.—New appointments.—King sends a letter to the Prince of Orange by Lord Feversham.—Rumours of different kinds.—Queen and Prince of Wales arrived at Ostend.—Princess Anne's entry into Oxford.—The King's final departure; and arrival of the Prince of Orange.

London, Dec. 19th, 1688.

SIR,

THE King returned on Saturday from Feversham to Rochester, and on Sunday about four in the afternoon came through the City, preceded by a great many gentlemen bareheaded, and followed by a numerous company with loud huzzas. The King stopped at the

Queen-dowager's before he came to White-hall, and the evening concluded with ringing of bells and bonfirés.

Those at Feversham, who rifled his Majesty of his money, &c. came with great conrition, and would have restored the same; but his Majesty not only refused to take it, but gave them ten guineas to drink his health.*

* " All these things were transacted, in the belief that he King had left the nation; and indeed he was gone rom Whitehall with that intention. He was got as far as a little place near Feversham, and had even embarked in a small vessel that was to carry him to a frigate ready to ransport him to France. This vessel not being able to sail immediately, by reason of a tempestuous wind, Sir Edward Hales, one of the King's attendants, sent his footman to the post-office at Feversham. His livery was known by a man, who told some others that Sir Edward was not far off. The footman was followed to the river-side, and seen to make signs to some people on board a bark; whereupon the fishermen and other persons of Feversham immediately boarded the vessel where the King was. Sir Edward was soon known; and the King, being taken for his chaplain, had many indignities put upon him. Then, searching him, they found four hundred guineas, and several valuable seals and jewels, which they took from him. Amongst the people who

The King, before his coming from Feversham, made the Lord Winchelsea* Lord Lieutenant of Kent, in the room of Lord Teynham,† as also Governor of Dover Castle.
His Majesty sending the Earl of Feversham with a letter to the Prince of Orange,
his Highness detained the said Earl for high
treason, declaring he did it for his disbanding

crowded into the ship, there happened to be a constable who
knew the King, and, throwing himself at his feet, begged
him to forgive the rudeness of the mob, and ordered restitution to be made of what had been taken from him. The
King received the jewels and the seals, but gave the four
hundred guineas among them. After this, he desired to be
gone ; but the people, by a sort of violence, conducted him
to a public inn in the town. Here he sent for the Earl
of Winchelsea, Lord Lieutenant of the county, who prevailed with him not to leave the kingdom, but to return
towards London."—Rapin.

* Heneage (Finch) second Earl of Winchilsea. After the
King's final departure, he was among the peers who voted
for the elevation of William and Mary to the throne. He
died in 1689.

† Christopher (Roper) fifth Lord Teynham. James
had made him Lord Lieutenant and Custos Rotulorum of
the County of Kent in 1687. He was a Roman Catholic.

he army without orders, &c. At which his Majesty was somewhat concerned.*

We had a general discourse that his Majesty would constitute the Prince of Orange Admiral and Generalissimo of all his three kingdoms. In effect it is almost done; for yesterday his Highness sent his orders to all the King's forces in and about London to march out to certain quarters, except only the Lord Craven's regiment, and six companies of the King's regiment to go and take possession of

He died at Brussels just at this time, which occasioned the vacancy in the Lord Lieutenancy.

* " Dec. 13th. Somebody told the Prince how Lord Feversham had disbanded the King's army; and that the soldiers were all running up and down, not knowing what course to take: at which the Prince seemed very angry at Lord Feversham, and said, ' I am not to be thus dealt with.'

" Dec. 16th, Sunday. Bentinck told me, the Prince was very angry with my Lord Feversham, and had committed him; that his Highness had answered the King's letter by Monsieur Zulestein, and desired his Majesty to stay at Rochester. I asked Bentinck, ' What could be the meaning of committing Lord Feversham?' To which he made me no answer; but with a shrug, ' Alas! my Lord.' This proceeding startles me."—Diary of Henry Earl of Clarendon.

Portsmouth, assigning the Irish therein other quarters and subsistence-money.

The Duke of Grafton has possessed himself of Tilbury fort, and the Irish are sent away with passes; but Captain Nugent is committed to Maidstone for beginning the late disorder.

Sunday last, Sir Wm. Waller* came to town, and was publicly at the coffee-house, church, and meeting; and the Lord Colchester, Col. Godfrey, and Sir Tho. Clarges,† who went to the Prince, are also in town.

* Sir William Waller was an active magistrate for the county of Middlesex, and a strenuous opposer of most of the measures of Charles the Second's Government. He was the only son of Sir William Waller, the celebrated Parliamentary General, by his second wife, Anne Finch, daughter of the first Earl of Winchilsea.

† Sir Thomas Clarges, Knight, was the brother-in-law of Monck, who raised him by his interest to fortune and consideration. Burnet says, " He was an honest but a haughty man. He became afterwards a very considerable Parliament-man, and valued himself on his opposing the Court, and on his frugality in managing the public money; for he had Cromwell's economy ever in his mouth, and was always for reducing the expense of war, to the modesty and parsimony of

The Prince has given the Earl of Oxford the Duke of Berwick's regiment of horse, which his Lordship was formerly Colonel of.

There came advice yesterday, that the Queen and Prince of Wales were safely arrived at Ostend in Flanders.

Yesterday, Sir Roger Lestrange* was seized

those times.   Many thought he carried this too far, but it made him very popular.   After he was become very rich himself by the public money, he seemed to take care that nobody else should grow as rich as he was in that way."   Sir Thomas's only son, Walter Clarges, was made a Baronet during his father's lifetime, in 1674.   Sir Thomas Clarges died Oct. 4th, 1695.

* Sir Roger L'Estrange, a most prolific writer of political tracts, and publisher of newspapers, was descended from an ancient family, and was born December 17th, 1616.   He suffered for the Royalist cause during the civil wars ; for which, after the Restoration, he was made Licenser of the Press, a lucrative situation, which he retained till the Revolution. He was besides this concerned in the publication of different public journals, and was the person who first set up the London Gazette, on the 4th of February, 1665.   At the Revolution he fell into trouble as a disaffected person ; and Queen Mary showed her dislike to him by the anagram of " Lying Strange Roger," which she made upon his name.   He died September 11th, 1704, in the eighty-eighth year of his age.

and brought before the Court of Aldermen, and upon oath made by one Mr. Braddon, of something in his writings tending against the Government, was committed to Newgate.

One Major Littleton and Captain Adderley quarrelled and fought a duel in the street, and the former was killed in the rencounter.

The Princess of Denmark made a splendid entry into Oxford, Saturday last; Sir John Laneer, with his regiment, meeting her Royal Highness some miles out of town. The Earl of Northampton,* with 500 horse, led the van. Her Royal Highness was preceded by the Bishop of London,† at the head of a noble troop of gentlemen; his Lordship riding in a purple cloak, martial habit, pistols before him, and his sword drawn; and his cornet had the inscription in golden letters on his standard,

* George (Compton) fourth Earl of Northampton, to whose house of Castle Ashby the Princess had fled when she left Whitehall. He received various marks of the favour of his Sovereigns, during the reigns of William, Anne, and George the First, and died April 15th, 1727.

† Compton.

Nolumus Leges Angliæ mutari. The rear was brought up by some militia troops. The Mayor and Aldermen in their formalities, met her at the North Gate; and the Vice Chancellor, attended by the heads of the University, in their scarlet gowns, made to her a speech in English; and the Prince received her Royal Highness at Christ Church quadrangle, with all possible demonstrations of love and affection; and they will be to-morrow at Windsor.

Last night the King went off from Court; and this day, about three o'clock, the Prince arrived at St. James's, with great acclamations of joy and huzzas.

The gentleman that writeth the news-letters being indisposed, desires to be excused for writing not himself this day.

For John Ellis, Esq. Secretary to the
    Commissioners for the Revenue of
    Ireland,   At Dublin.

CCXXXIX.

Foreign news.—Details respecting the King's departure, and
the Prince of Orange's arrival.—One of the Prince of
Orange's guards killed, &c.

London, December 20th, 1688.
SIR,

WE had on Tuesday two Dutch mails :
the latter tells us of the death of Pensionary
Fagell,* well known in England for his letter
to Mr. Steward.

The province of Holland has at length con-

* Gaspar Fagel, an eminent Dutch statesman, and supporter
of the House of Orange.   He was born at Haarlem in 1629,
and pursued for some time the study of the law.   In 1670,
he was named "Greffier" of the States General, a post which
continued to be exercised by his family till the French Revolution.   In 1672, he succeeded the unhappy De Witt, as
Grand Pensionary.   He was engaged with great success in
all the political transactions of the time, in which the interests of his country were concerned.   But his great work
was the arrangement and contrivance of William's expedition to England.   The success of this he did not live to see,
as he died December 15th, 1688, at which period the news of
the great event had not reached Holland.

ented to the raising a hundred troops of horse,
ixty men in each.   The French having made a
kind of blockade round Mastricht, were driven
away by Prince Waldeck, killing about 400;
and the said Prince has taken by assault Reins-
burgh, and put all the French therein to the
sword.   A person was arrested at the Hague
'or publishing of false news, and upon examination they find him to be a spy sent by Cardinal
Furstemberg.   They have whipped him with
a rope about his neck, and committed him for
two years to the Rasp-house.   They write from
Hambourgh that, on the 17th, 5000 Swedes
embarked on the Duchy of Bremen for Holland.

  The Dauphin is come to Luxemburgh ; and
Monsieur de Monbrun is gone to Brussells, to
demand a passage for the French troops to
make war against Holland, which being refused, war will be declared against Spain.   The
Emperor has resolved to declare a perpetual
war against the French King ; and the Confederates are to have in the spring an army of

80,000 men in a body, without reckoning the forces of the Emperor.

The Swiss have granted the Emperor to raise 15,000 men in their territories. The French King has taken or borrowed 500,000 livres more of the Bank of Paris, to carry on his war.

The Marquis d Albyville, the King's Envoy in Holland, has published a book, by which he would prove the Prince of Wales to be the legitimate son of the King his master.

The Bishop of Munster has at last declared for the Emperor, and promised to send 9000 men to the army of the Allies, in case of need.

What we may add to the King's last withdrawing from Whitehall is, that the Marquis Halifax, Earl of Shrewsbury, and the Lord Delamere, arrived at Whitehall on Tuesday, about twelve o'clock, and brought the King the message to retire the same day either to Hampton Court, or somewhere else ; signifying that the Prince did not think it safe for him to come to London, so long as his Majesty had such a confluence of Papists still about him, and that the Prince's Guards should go along with him to preserve him from the insults of the *mobile*. The King went accordingly at one o'clock, and lay that night at one Mr. Eckins's house, an attorney in Gravesend, and about ten next morning set forwards for Rochester. His Majesty's barge was followed by ten or twelve boats of the Prince's soldiers.

The Prince of Orange remains at St. James's, where no great business was done yesterday, by reason of paying and receiving visits; only a regiment was sent to possess themselves of the Tower. Most of the Bishops about the town were with his Highness. The Duke of Norfolk came and paid his devoirs. The Prince in the afternoon went to Whitehall, and from thence in the Queen's barge to Somerset-house, to compliment the Queen-dowager. In his return, hearing that the Prince and Princess of Denmark were come to town, called to see them at the Cockpit.

One Captain St. Ange, a French Roman Catholic, was seized at Court, and sent prisoner to Newgate.

The garrison of Portsmouth quietly submitted to the order of the Prince, and drew thereout ; and the Duke of Berwick rendered himself to the Lord Dartmouth on board the fleet. Colonel Talmash is said to be made Governor of the said place by the Prince.

A minister in the City is made one of the Prince's Chaplains.   Mr. Ferguson goes publicly to the coffee-houses.

It is said, an order will suddenly be published, to banish all Papists ten miles out of town.

One of the Prince's guards was found in Long Acre with his throat cut, and other wounds about him ; and being known that he quartered in a Papist's house near that place, the people are secured upon it.*

* Reresby, who appears to have been somewhat of a Jacobite, gives the following unfavourable description of William's army.—" January 22d, 1689.   And now being at liberty to go where I pleased, I repaired to London, where being arrived, I was presently sensible of a great alteration ; the

The Lord Teynham and Mr. Richard Lee*
are seized, and sent to Upner Castle prisoners.
The Earl of Feversham is put in the round
Tower in Windsor Castle.

For John Ellis, Esq. Secretary to the
   Commissioners for the Revenue of
   Ireland,   At Dublin.

CCXL.

London, Dec. 29th, 1688.

THE 24th of last month was the date
of your's to me : many transactions, you may
be sure, have passed here ; the prints are so full
of them, that I will say the less in this way. I

Guards, and other parts of the army, which both for their
persons and gallantry were an ornament to the place, were
sent to quarter at a distance, while the streets swarmed with
ill-favoured and ill-accoutred Dutchmen, and other strangers
of the Prince's army ; and yet the city seemed to be mightily
pleased with their deliverers, nor perceived their deformity,
or the oppression they laboured under, by far more unsup-
portable than ever they had suffered from the English."

* Probably a brother of the first Lord Lichfield.

wish you here for many reasons. The King landed on Tuesday morning near Marquès, and went post to Paris on Wednesday.＊ I cannot see who your government will fall to : I think neither our friend, nor the pert pretender. The Prince is very unwilling to break any one regiment ; so that he must have farther work ere long for them. I know not what will be my lot ; but I am vain enough to think, in a general bustle I shall shift for one : you will pardon me that I say no more.

＊ " On the 23d of December, at three in the morning, the King privately withdrew from Rochester, taking with him the Duke of Berwick, his natural son, Mr. Skelton, and Abadie, and went on horseback to a place near the river, where he embarked on a small frigate, which landed him safely at Ambleteuse in France, from whence he repaired to St. Germain's."—Rapin.

INDEX.

THE END.

LONDON :
PRINTED BY S. AND R. BENTLEY,
Dorset Street, Fleet Street.

3 2044 005 033 7

Check Out More Titles From HardPress Classics Series In this collection we are offering thousands of classic and hard to find books. This series spans a vast array of subjects – so you are bound to find something of interest to enjoy reading and learning about.

Subjects:
Architecture
Art
Biography & Autobiography
Body, Mind &Spirit
Children & Young Adult
Dramas
Education
Fiction
History
Language Arts & Disciplines
Law
Literary Collections
Music
Poetry
Psychology
Science
…and many more.

Visit us at www.hardpress.net

CPSIA information can be obtained
at www.ICGtesting.com
Printed in the USA
BVHW080815270819

556819BV00011B/2276/P